AF414188

Toxic Pulpit

Carl Davis

Published by Carl Davis, 2024.

While every precaution has been taken in the preparation of this book, the publisher assumes no responsibility for errors or omissions, or for damages resulting from the use of the information contained herein.

TOXIC PULPIT

First edition. January 18, 2024.

Copyright © 2024 Carl Davis.

ISBN: 979-8224008032

Written by Carl Davis.

Also by Carl Davis

Ek, is Dawid Soeker
A Brief History Of Christianity In Africa
Icing the Eskimo - The Art of Aggressive Sales
Introduction to Pastoral Counselling
Nuclear Faith
Toxic Pulpit
Van Paradegrond tot Pastorie
Group Dynamics and Motivation
Introduction to Leadership and Management
Pastoral counselling models for perinatal and postpartum episodes
Basic New Testament Survey
Help! I'm managing personnel
So......You want to be a Waiter
The Art of Preaching
Eternal Logos: The Evolution of Scriptural Interpretation: From
Ancient Methodology to Postmodern Perspectives
Ewige Woord Die Evolusie van Skrifuitleg: Van Antieke Metodiek tot
Postmoderne Perspektiewe
Teaching Ministry
The Funny Side Of Reasoning - Fallacies, principles and typologies in
the modern business world.
Passion Unleashed: Igniting The Future With Purpose.

Toxic Pulpit

A Survival Guide to coping with Narcissistic Church Leadership

1

All Rights Reserved
Dr. Carl J Davis
South Africa
2023

Toxic Pulpit: A Survival Guide to Coping with Narcissistic Church Leadership

Embark on a transformative journey with "Toxic Pulpit," a guide that empowers you to break free from the clutches of narcissistic leaders using cognitive-behavioral strategies.

Inside the Pages:

- Uncover patterns of manipulation and regain control of your narrative.
- Challenge distorted thoughts with practical cognitive restructuring techniques.
- Establish unshakable boundaries and communicate assertively.

Empowering Solutions:

- Discover mindfulness and relaxation techniques for resilience.
- Develop coping strategies to navigate stress with grace.
- Learn assertive communication skills to reclaim your voice.

Community and Support:

- Seek support from colleagues and friends who understand your journey.
- Explore professional help to guide you through the process.

Exit with Confidence:

- Strategically plan your exit while focusing on self-empowerment.
- Navigate legal considerations with confidence and knowledge.

Regain Control of Your Narrative:

- "Toxic Pulpit" is your roadmap to freedom, guiding you through self-validation, empowerment, and a healthier, more fulfilling life.

Take the first step towards reclaiming your life. Break free from toxic leadership with "Toxic Pulpit" – your guide to resilience and empowerment. #ToxicPulpit #BreakFree #EmpowermentJourney

Chapter 1: The Narcissistic Leader

The Profile of a Narcissist in a Leadership Role: Psychological Dangers and Harmful Influence

A narcissist is not just an individual with an excess of self-love; It is a personality disorder that can have a profound impact on interpersonal relationships and leadership abilities. When these characteristics are integrated into a leadership context, the psychological dangers and harmful influence can worsen dramatically. This is even more dangerous if he or she is in church leadership or, even worse, the church pastor!

Ten qualities of a narcissistic church leader

1. **Excessive need for admiration:** He or she constantly seeks praise and worship from followers, with an insatiable desire for affirmation. As we will see later, this stems from a lack of self-worth.

A narcissist has an inexplicable craving for constant admiration and recognition. This need can lead to an unhealthy dependence on the loyalty of his followers.

A narcissist shows an excess of self-appreciation and sees himself as exceptionally fit for leadership. This excessive self-glorification leads to a lack of empathy for other views and needs.

1. **Lack of empathy for others:** The person has difficulty understanding or caring for the feelings and needs of those around them and often prioritizes their own agenda. They cannot understand that others have issues that need to be addressed. Helping others may remove the focus off the

narcissist.

Empathy, an essential emotional connection to others, is a weakness for a narcissist. This often manifests itself as an inability to acknowledge the suffering or needs of community members.

1. **Exploitative Behavior:** Such a person will be taking advantage of others to achieve personal goals by using their position for personal gain. People will be exploited and manipulated to further the plans and the goals of a narcissist.

A narcissist often uses people to achieve his own goals without regard to the well-being of others. This exploitation can be physical, emotional, or even financial.

1. **Sense of Justice:** They believe they inherently deserve special treatment and privileges without necessarily earning them. Again, the needs of others will always be inferior to the needs of a narcissist.
2. **Preoccupation with fantasies of limitless success:** They are engaged with grandiose daydreams of unparalleled achievement, often separate from reality. They will even run their ministry into the ground to achieve their grandiose fantasies. Any stress on the church caused by them will be deflected to the congregants, who must pick up the pieces and follow the dream and vision.
3. **Belief in Their Unique Interest:** Seeing themselves as extraordinarily special or better than others fosters a sense of elitism. They do not have time to earn respect, yet they will demand respect, even if it means using their title(s) or status.
4. **Manipulative Tendencies:** Use cunning and deceit to control or influence others, often for personal gain. It is not out of

the ordinary for a narcissist to manipulate, twist, and non-contextualize Scripture to manipulate the congregants.

He or she may include tactics such as gaslighting, where the reality of community members is denied or distorted.

1. **Difficulty maintaining healthy relationships:** They have difficulty forming genuine connections, as relationships are often transactional and revolve around the leader's needs. Relationships may be tied, or untied as necessary, to the will of the narcissist. Anyone who can no longer contribute or manipulate will be discarded.

2. **Envy of others or belief that others are envious of them:** Feel resentful of others' success or see that others are envious of their perceived greatness. This is again a reflection of the low self-esteem and self-worth of the narcissist. Anyone succeeding in life will be treated with envy as it takes the focus from the narcissist.

3. **Arrogant and haughty behavior:** Show a condescending and superior attitude, reject the opinions of others, and assert dominance.

The longing to be superior often emerges as arrogance and an unwavering belief in one's

Psychological Dangers of a Narcissist in Leadership:
1. Emotional exhaustion:
Community members may feel emotionally exhausted due to the constant pressure to meet the narcissist's needs and expectations. This emotional exhaustion can lead to anxiety, depression, and even health problems. This is even more prominent in a Christian environment where spiritual anxiety and depression may occur.
2. Confusion and Identity Loss:

A narcissist can create a sphere of confusion through constant changes in the interpretation of community values and identity. This confusion can lead to a loss of individual identity within the community. This is mainly done as a show of power and control.

3. Lack of Trust:

A narcissist in a leadership role often creates an environment of distrust. Community members tend to constantly doubt their own judgment and decision-making. The narcissist does not trust anyone except him/herself. Even family members will not be trusted as they are closer to knowing the real reason a narcissist functions the way he or she does.

4. Social Isolation:

The urge for dominance and the repudiation of other views can lead to social isolation within the community. This isolation increases dependence on the narcissist as the sole source of information and guidelines. In the church environment, this is achieved by isolating the church members from society or other churches. Those not toe the line will be shunned or expelled from the social group.

5. Suppression of Criticism:

A narcissist in a leadership role will tend to suppress and deny criticism. This prevents a healthy and constructive sphere where criticism can be seen as an opportunity for growth. He or she cannot belive that they are fallible. For them, mistakes are unknown; any mistakes will be shifted to others. Admitting errors is to acknowledge fallibility. Blame moving or finding other faults is someone will counter where errors are made by the narcissist.

6. Spiritual and Emotional Void:

Community members may experience a sense of spiritual and emotional emptiness because the narcissist can divert the community's focus from the deeper meaning of their faith to a superficial admiration of the leader. Congregants may feel that they have sin in their lives and are spiritually immature. Disappointing the narcissist is tantamount to offending God Himself.

The Influence of Narcissism on Work Environments: Challenges and Implications

Introduction:

Narcissism, as a personality disorder characterized by an excess of selfishness, lack of empathy, and an intense need for admiration, can have a considerable impact on various work environments. Let us explore the challenges and implications of narcissism across multiple working positions, focusing on its influence on the individual himself and the environment within which they function.

1. Life Art or Therapeutic Professions:

The life art and therapeutic professions, which require individuals to have a profound empathy and understanding of others' emotional states, can be a complex environment for narcissists to function effectively. These professions call for clinical skills and the ability to display genuine, thoughtful empathy. Narcissists, with their focus on self and lack of empathy, may struggle to establish a meaningful and therapeutic relationship with clients or patients. The constant need for admiration and a tendency to direct the conversation to themselves can disturb the therapeutic dynamics and create an unhealthy atmosphere.

2. Leadership positions without Appropriate Control:

In environments where leadership requires a balanced approach and is not founded on excess self-glorification, narcissists may struggle to be influential leaders. Positions where a democratic or collaborative-oriented leadership style is needed, can be problematic for narcissists who often see their own views as the only rights. The inability to value the opinions of others, combined with a need for unlimited admiration, can lead to a dysfunctional work environment where the group's interests are not adequately considered.

3. Collective or Collaboration-Oriented Environments:

Work environments aimed at collaboration and developing a positive corporate culture can be an obstacle for narcissists. The tool point of a narcissist's attention to one's own interests and the tendency to use others for personal gain contributes to an environment in which cooperation is difficult. A collective approach to problem-solving and decision-making can cause conflict with the self-centered nature of narcissists, which can be a potential source of tension within the work environment.

4. Empathic Professions:

Occupations that require a high degree of empathy and sensitivity towards others, such as social work, can be a challenge for narcissists. This is also true of those in Ministry, yet many narcissists may end up in ministry. The lack of a genuine interest in the needs and emotions of others can lead to inappropriate interactions and a lack of practical assistance. Focusing on self can also be a barrier to building a trusting relationship with clients or patients, which is critical for success in these professions.

5. Occupations That Require Uncertainty:

Work environments where uncertainty, experimentation, or change are a part of the day-to-day dynamic may be complex for narcissists to navigate. The need for control and security, typical of narcissistic personality disorder, may conflict with the dynamic nature of occupations in which uncertainty is a feature. These narcissistic tendencies can lead to resistance to change and stagnation within the work environment.

6. Positions Where Personal Criticism Plays a Major Role:

In environments where feedback is a part of the day-to-day dynamics and personal criticism often occurs, narcissists may struggle to cope with these situations. The sensitivity to criticism and a tendency to react defensively can create an atmosphere of fear of criticism. This may impede personal and professional growth within the work environment.

7. Long-term collaborations:

Building long-lasting, intimate relationships in personal or professional contexts may be a challenge for narcissists. Their tendency to use people for personal gain and a lack of genuine interest in others' well-being can lead to a lack of trust and respect within the relationship. This can impede successfully maintaining durable relationships within the work environment.

8. Empowering-Leading Environments:

In environments where the goal is to empower individuals and provide opportunities for growth and development, narcissists may struggle to maintain a climate of shared empowerment. The constant need for admiration and a focus on self-interest can lead to an imbalance in power relations within the team, increasing the potential for development

The Pernicious Influence of a Narcissist in Leadership:

1. Community Fragmentation:

A narcissist may cause community fragmentation by sowing division and conflict. This can lead to a lack of solidarity and decrease the community's overall well-being.

2. Loss of Community Goals:

The obsession with one's interests and needs can lead to neglecting the community's original goals and values.

3. Discouragement of True Spirituality:

A narcissist in a leadership role can discourage the community from pursuing true spirituality by shifting the focus to glorifying the leader himself.

4. Harmful Environmental Culture:

The culture created by a narcissist can be harmful to the mental and emotional well-being of community members. This culture can promote aggression, fear, and a lack of fellow humanity.

5. Loss of Creative Contributions:

A narcissist may discourage the creative contributions of community members by creating an atmosphere of control and a lack of appreciation for variety.

6. Long-term emotional damage:

The long-term impact of a narcissist in leadership includes potential emotional damage that is difficult to repair. Community members may lose their ability to function emotionally stable.

Example 1: Jim Jones and the Jonestown Tragedy

A charismatic and manipulative leader, Jim Jones founded the Peoples Temple and built a community of followers in Jonestown, Guyana. Jones created a self-imposed sacred status for himself, in which he was considered the only leader. The community was built around Jones' social justice ideology but increasingly adopted a totalitarian structure.

Jones physically, emotionally, and even sexually abused his followers while at the same time creating an atmosphere of fear and control. His narcissistic desire for absolute power led to the tragic Jonestown Massacre in 1978. At his command, more than 900 people, including children, committed suicide by ingesting poison. This event stands as a glaring example of the devastating effect of a narcissistic leader on a community.

Example 2: Adolf Hitler and the Third Reich

Adolf Hitler, as the leader of Nazi rule, is a synonym for the malignant effect of a narcissistic leader on an entire nation. Hitler projected his own delusions of racial superiority and German mastery, which eventually led to the Holocaust and World War II.

Hitler's inability to accept criticism, his contempt for other races, and his obsession with a utopian German empire led the nation into a campaign of terror and destruction. His narcissistic urge for admiration and his irresponsible decision-making led the German community to catastrophic ruin.

Example 3: Charles Manson and the Manson Family

Charles Manson, a criminal with a disproportionate need for control, formed a sect-like community known as the Manson family. Manson convinced his followers he was a messiah, encouraging a pirate philosophy of apocalyptic violence.

In 1969, members of the Manson family brutally murdered eight people, including pregnant actress Sharon Tate, on his orders. Manson's narcissistic urge for control and his ability to manipulate his followers led to a series of brutal murders that shocked American society.

Example 4: Pol Pot and the Rode Khmer

Pol Pot, the leader of the Communist Party of Kampuchea (Cambodia), pursued a utopian vision of an agrarian society. However, his policies ushered in the Rode Khmer period, which was marked by mass extermination, torture, and the destruction of intellectual and urban communities.

Pol Pot's narcissistic craving for a historical legacy led to the deaths of an estimated two million people through murder, torture, and starvation. This period of absolute control and cruelty tore apart the Cambodian community for decades after the Khmer Rode Fall in the 1970s.

Concluding Thoughts: The Devastating Effects of Narcissistic Leadership

These historical examples of narcissistic leadership illustrate the devastating effect this personality disorder can have on communities. The inability to accept criticism, the urge for control, and an unhealthy self-appreciation can lead to tragic outcomes and the downfall of entire communities. This highlights the critical importance of vigilance and resistance to the rise of such leaders, as well as the need for awareness about the psychological dangers that come with this form of leadership.

A narcissist in a leadership role brings a complex dynamic to a community. The psychological dangers and harmful influences that arise from this emphasize the need for awareness and intervention to maintain a healthy and supportive environment. Communities must be alert to the signs of a narcissistic leader and ready to implement effective strategies to limit its adverse effects and promote recovery.

Chapter 2 – Narcissistic Cult leaders often surround themselves with "yes men" or people who show unconditional loyalty to strengthen their position of authority and control.

For the purpose of this chapter, we will look at the role of a narcissistic leader within a cult.

The narcissist, especially within a cilt environment, will always surround him/herself with self-appointed "yes men." Here are some reasons why they might do this:

Lack of Opposition: Cult leaders often don't want to be confronted with opposing opinions or criticism. By having people around them who see them as "yes men," they ensure little or no resistance to their decisions or ideas.

- Lack of opposition within a cult environment is often a strategy cult leaders use to maintain a controlled and obedient followership.

Here are some ways in which this dynamic manifests itself:

- **Criticism meets resistance:** Cult leaders rarely tolerate criticism or opposing opinions within the group. Any challenge can be viewed as a threat to the leader's authority and the cult's ideology.
- **Self-censorship by members:** Members of the cult can apply self-censorship to protect themselves from the possible negative consequences of expressing dissenting opinions. This self-censorship contributes to a climate in which individuals suppress their true thoughts and views.

- **Punishment for opposition:** If someone within the cult dares to voice opposition, there may be punitive measures, such as public humiliation, isolation, or even exclusion from the group. These negative consequences dissuade members from expressing any form of opposition.
- **Ideological Conformity:** Cult leaders strive to completely conform to the cult's ideological framework. Any deviation from this framework is discouraged and often perceived as a sign of bad faith or betrayal.
- **Spiritual Pressure:** The cult environment can exert intense pressure on individuals to show agreement with the leader and this assent on a spiritual level. These pressures can lead to a more profound emotional commitment to the cult leader and his teachings.
- The lack of opposition creates an environment where a singular and often deformed view of reality can flourish. This strengthens the cult leader's control over members' thought processes and makes it harder for individuals to make objective decisions or consider alternative perspectives. This dynamic of a closed system may increase the potential for abuse and manipulation within the cult.

Affirmation of Authority: A cult leader's authority and self-esteem may depend on unconditional loyalty. People who repeatedly affirm their views help feed the leader's ego and reinforce their belief that they are infallible.

Affirmation of authority within a cult environment is a strategic practice used by cult leaders to create an atmosphere of absolute obedience and loyalty.

This dynamic can manifest itself in several ways:

- **Unconditional Loyalty:** Cult leaders often expect unquestioning loyalty from their followers. This loyalty is shown to the cult as a whole and, above all, to the leader's person. Any doubt about the leader's authority can be perceived as a betrayal of the cult's goals.

- **Adoration of the Leader:** The cult leader can be considered glorified and adorable. This worship is not limited to spiritual worship. Still, it can manifest in other aspects of the followers' lives, including personal decisions and interactions.
- **Strengthening Ego:** Cult leaders' egos are often reinforced by the constant affirmation of their authority. Positive feedback, praise, and glorifying the leader as an exceptional or divine figure nourish the leader's self-esteem.
- **Increased privileges:** If affirmation of authority has been achieved, the leader may experience increased privacy and liberties. These privileges can range from financial favoritism to exclusive access to information, affirming the leader as the central power figure.
- **Dehumanization of Critics:** Persons who do not agree with the leader's authority or criticize can be dehumanized. These people are often perceived as hostile to the cult's goals or the persona of a narcissist, and any opposition to the leader is interpreted as a personal attack.
- **Mythological Status:** The leader can be assigned a mythical or supernatural status within the cult community. This exceptional and high-status award reinforces the idea that the leader is infallible and superior to ordinary people.

This affirmation of authority is an essential tool for maintaining the cult's structure and its leader's domination. This affects not only the behavior of the followers within the group but also their self-perception and identity concerning the leader and the cult.

Reducing Threat: A cult leader may fear internal rebellion or betrayal. The leader tries to minimize the potential threat from within by approaching only people who confirm their loyalty.

Reducing threats within a cult environment is a strategic goal that the cult leader pursues to maintain a sense of security, control, and stability within the group. (The same can be said of a narcissistic leader) Here's how this dynamic of reduced threat can manifest:

- **Elimination of Opposition:** One of the priJane objectives is to eliminate any form of opposition or opposition to the leader's authority. This can be done by creating an atmosphere in which criticism or doubt is considered unacceptable and where people apply self-censorship so as not to enter into opposition.

- **Suppression of Critical Thinking:** Cult leaders often aim to suppress critical thinking within the community. Individuals are encouraged not to criticize and to hide any questions or doubts. This suppression of critical thinking prevents members from considering alternative perspectives.

- **Spiritual Belief of Infallibility:** Cult leaders can foster a culture of infallibility, where the leader is perceived as infallible and his or her teaching as the only actual truth. This belief reinforces the idea that there is no outside threat since the leader is perceived as an omniscient divine authority.

- **Creating an "Us against Them" Mentality:** To unite the group, a cult leader can foster an "us against them" mentality. The outside world and anyone not belonging to the cult can be perceived as a threat. This dynamic reinforces a closed unit within the community.

- **Anxiety field:** Cult leaders can create a climate of fear in which members don't feel safe to criticize or ask questions. The threat of potential negative consequences, such as punishment or isolation, can prompt members to self-censor their thoughts and decisions.

- **Control of Information: Cult** leaders can control the flow of information to promote only those views and ideas favorable to the Cult. Alternative communication or critical perspectives may be limited or excluded.

These strategies aim to create an illusion of a threat-free environment within the cult, leading to a total commitment to the leader and the ideological framework of the group. This reduced threat contributes to a deeper degree of control and loyalty within the cult community.

Control over information: " Yes-men" contribute to managing information within the cult. This helps to maintain a one-sided and centralized view of reality, as opposing views or criticisms are often eliminated.

Checking information within a cult environment is critical to the leader's strategy to control the followers' thoughts, beliefs, and perceptions.

Here's how these information control dynamics often manifest themselves:

- **Selective Information:** Cult leaders may communicate information to advance a specific narrative. This means that members only have access to information favorable to the cult's perspective while excluding or minimizing critical or opposing information.
- **Disinformation:** Cult leaders can use willful disinformation to spread false information or deform reality to adapt it to the cult's ideological framework. This tactic serves to promote a deformed perception of truth within the group.
- **Limited Access to External Information:** Members of the cult may be discouraged or even barred from having access to

information from outside the cult. This limitation of external information prevents members from being exposed to alternative perspectives contrary to the cult's teachings.

- **Control over Communication:** Cult leaders may control the internal communication channels within the group. This control includes monitoring company groups, emails, and even personal parties to maintain a unity of messages and eliminate potential opposition.
- **Punishment for Offence:** Members who attempt to bring in alternative information or challenge the cult leader's narrative may be exposed to punitive measures. These punishments can include isolation, public humiliation, or even exclusion from the community.
- **Control of Teaching and Training:** Cult leaders may retain a monopoly over teaching and training within the cult. This means that only the leader's view of truth is correct, and other perspectives are discouraged or discouraged.

This control over information serves some goals within the cult, including maintaining the leader's authority, strengthening a uniform group identity, and preventing internal dissension. However, it can also lead to a limited view of reality within the cult community and a lack of objective view of matters.

Validation of Decisions: A cult leader's decisions are often viewed as the final and only correct path. Creating an environment of consenting believers allows the leader's decisions to be validated and seen as indisputable.

Validation of decisions within a cult environment is a process in which the leader's choices and guidelines are considered absolutely correct, without questioning or opposing.

This is done by:

- **Infallibility of the Leader:** The cult leader is often viewed as infallible, and his or her decisions are accepted as the only correct choices. This belief strengthens the leader's authority and creates a climate in which doubts or questioning around decisions are discouraged.

- **Centralized Decision** Making: In a cult community, the decision-making process may be centralized around the leader. The leader often makes all crucial decisions without allowing the thorough participation of other members. This centralized process validates the leader's authority and eliminates alternative perspectives.

- **Lack of Democracy:** A cult may lack democratic processes in which members do not have the right to actively participate in decision-making. The leader's will is law; questioning this will be considered rebellion.

- **Punishment for Questions:** If a member of the cult questions the leader's decisions, punishment may follow. This punishment can take several forms, including public humiliation, isolation, or exclusion. These measures act as a deterrent against any form of opposition.

- **Belief in a Divine Direction:** The leader's decisions are often viewed as an outgrowth of a divine direction. This belief reinforces the idea that there is no room for human doubt or questions because the leader is led by a higher power.

- **Uniformity in Thinking:** Validation of Decisions promotes a uniform way of thinking within the Cult. Reading consent and obedience to the leader's decisions are essential to the individual's spiritual well-being within the group.

This ratification of decisions creates an environment where the leader's authority is unquestionable, and members hesitate to consider alternative perspectives. This often leads to a sphere of self-censorship and a lack of critical thinking within the cult community.

Control Over Narrative: A cult leader may want to control the group's narrative to promote a specific image of himself or herself and the cult. This can be a strategy to influence the outside world's perception.

Control over the narrative in a cult environment is a strategic attempt by the leader to manipulate how the cult and its goals are perceived.

This is done by:

- **Writing the History:** A cult leader may reinterpret the group's history to promote a specific narrative that validates his or her authority. Past incidents can be rewritten to illustrate the leader's wisdom or divine guidance.

- **Discrediting Adversaries:** People or groups outside the cult who oppose the leader may be denied or demonized. These individuals or groups are often presented as hostile to the cult's goals, fostering an "us against them" mentality.

- **Dominance of Communication Channels:** Cult leaders may exercise control over the priJane communication channels within the group. This includes controlling social media, internal publications, and other sources of information. This control ensures that only the desired narrative comes outward.

- **Promoting an Ideal Image:** The leader can create an ideal image of himself or herself as a divine or exceptional figure. This ideal serves as an aim of veneration and worship within the cult community.

- **Determining Community Norms:** The leader often significantly influences the norms and values within the cult. These norms are determined by the narrative proclaimed by the leader, and any deviation from these norms can be considered rebellion and therefor classified as sin.

- **Re-Creation of Reality:** The leader can create an alternate reality by promoting a deformed view of events and facts. This distortion of reality aims to validate the leader's authority and manipulate members' perceptions of reality.

Control over the narrative serves not only to strengthen the leader's authority but also to promote a closed unity within the cult community. Members exposed to a one-way statement of information run the risk of adopting a one-sided view of reality and applying self-censorship per the prescribed narrative.

This dynamic of a closed and consenting inner circle can strengthen the leader's grip on the cult. Still, it can also lead to a lack of creativity, objective assessment of situations, and, ultimately, an unhealthy and disrupted environment within the cult.

Chapter 3: Distorted Interpretation of the Word: The Psychological Impact of Cherry-Picking and Distortion of Symbolic Texts

Introduction:

The interpretation of sacred texts profoundly impacts the faith and practice of a community. When a leader selects scripture verses and distorts symbolic texts, it can cause psychological disorientation within the community.

This chapter explores the psychological dangers of cherry-picking and the distortion of metaphors and allegories within the context of religious leadership.

1. Selective Bible Interpretation as an Instrument of Control:

Narcissistic leaders in the church often use a selective interpretation of the Bible to further their own agenda and maintain a power differential between themselves and their followers. These leaders can use specific Bible verses out of context, focus selectively on those parts of Scripture that affirm their authority, and discourage any form of opposition or question marks.

The leader uses the Bible as an instrument of control by convincing the followers that his interpretation is the only correct one, and any deviation from it is blasphemy or rebellion against God Himself. This approach reinforces the narcissistic leader's authority as the unique mediator between the believers and God, so any criticism of the leader or his teaching can be viewed as an attack on God's will.

The narcissistic leader's selective Bible interpretation feeds a culture of blind obedience, where followers hear only the selected portions of Scripture that advance the leader's agenda. This makes it difficult for the followers to have a complete and nuanced understanding of the Bible and can strengthen their dependence on the leader.

2. Use of Bible verses for personal self-publicity:

Narcissistic leaders may use Bible verses to promote personal anointing publicity and emphasize their divine calling. These leaders may quote specific Scripture verses that they consider a kind of divine chosen one and affirm their leadership as untouchable.

For example, a narcissistic leader might quote a Bible verse mentioning a prophecy about leadership with enthusiasm and present it as evidence of his divine chosenness. Using the Bible to soothe one's ego promotes a culture where followers see the leader as a spiritual guide and a religious entity elevated above criticism.

This approach allows the leader to enforce unqualified obedience from the followers since any opposition is perceived as an assault on the leader's divine position. Misusing the Bible in this way distorts the genuine purpose of spiritual guidance. It places the narcissistic leader at the center of the religious experience of the followers.

3. Misuse of text layout for personal gain:

Narcissistic leaders can use textual layout as a tactic to promote their own personal gain and manipulate followers. These leaders may take Bible verses out of context, give one-sided interpretations, or even construct false doctrines based on distorting Scriptural principles.

For example, a narcissistic leader might use a text that deals with the gift of leadership in the community and distort it to justify a view of unlimited, unqualified power and authority for himself. He may present the idea of submission as a divine commandment but requires it only of his followers and not of himself. This misuse of textual layout indicates a pathological desire to maintain one's interests, power, and control at the expense of the followers. The leader uses the Bible as a tool of manipulation to falsify the believers' understanding of the faith and place them in a position of dependence.

4. Instrumentalizing Use of Religion for Self-Glorification:

Narcissistic leaders may instrumentalize religion for self-glorification by using the Bible as a podium for the display of their own supposed divine power and wisdom. These leaders may use Bible stories and verses to emphasize their accomplishments, even when inconsistent with the original context.

For example, a narcissistic leader may quote a Bible verse about divine healing and use it to justify his own miraculous acts of healing. This misuse of the Bible presents the leader as a divine mediator of miracles, which puts the followers under pressure to glorify and obey him.

The instrumentalization of religion for self-glorification undermines the genuine spiritual values of humility, servitude, and devotion to God. This puts the narcissistic leader in a central position in the faith, where his own ego and desires are the priority.

5. Use of threats and promises as a manipulative agent:

Narcissistic leaders can use threats and promises from the Bible to keep followers in a state of constant dependence and fear. These leaders may quote Scripture verses describing the punishment of God for rebellion and disobedience and use them as a warning against those who do not obey blindly.

For example, a narcissistic leader may quote a Bible verse about the eternal consequences of sins to threaten and manipulate followers. This tactic creates a climate of fear and uncertainty within the community, in which individuals see themselves as dependent on the leader's care and protection.

The leader uses the Bible as an instrument of manipulation by presenting divine authority as a threatening force while simultaneously using the promise of salvation and prosperity to ensure obedience. This approach keeps followers in a psychological stranglehold, where they must suppress their own judgment and perceptions to conform to the supposed divine will of the leader.

1. **Cherry-Picking Verses:** Narcissistic leaders can selectively use verses that seem to support their authority while ignoring

contradictory passages. For example, they may emphasize verses about submission and unquestioning obedience while neglecting those who promote love and equality within the Christian community.

2. **Distortion of metaphors and allegories:** Misinterpretation involves manipulating symbolic language. A narcissistic leader can distort the metaphor of the "narrow gate" (Matthew 7:13-14), presenting it as an exclusive endorsement of their sect rather than a call to a righteous life.

3. **Elevate Personal Experiences to Scripture:** Leaders can interweave personal experiences with divine revelations. For example, a narcissistic leader might claim that a vivid dream or personal conviction is tantamount to biblical scriptures, leading followers to prioritize the leader's experiences over the actual teachings of the Bible.

4. **Ignoring historical and cultural context:** Disregarding historical and cultural context can lead to misinterpretation. For example, a leader might take a verse like "I can do all things through Christ who strengthens me" (Philippians 4:13), ignore Paul's specific circumstances, and turn it into a prosperity gospel mantra.

5. **Claim exclusive interpretation:** A narcissistic leader may claim that only they possess an accurate interpretation of the Bible. For example, they may claim unique insights into complex theological concepts, discouraging followers from consulting other theologians or scholars.

6. **Reinterpreting Traditional Theology:** By Misinterpreting Foundational Theology, Leaders can reshape Doctrine. For example, a leader might redefine the concept of salvation, emphasizing obedience to their authority rather than the traditional Christian understanding of grace through faith.

Cherry-Picking Versions:

A narcissistic leader often uses cherry-picking as a strategy to manipulate scripture and support his own agenda. This selective use of scripture involves selecting specific texts consistent with the leader's views while ignoring or minimizing other texts. The impact of this is twofold: first, it creates a deformed picture of the religious teachings within the community, and second, it creates a dependence on the leader as the sole source of interpretation.

Psychological Impact of Cherry-Picking:

1. **Loss of Credibility:** The community's credibility in the leader can be shaken when they realize that not all scripture is honored and accepted. This can lead to doubts about the leader's faith, sincerity, and integrity of the religious teachings.

2. **Emotional Conflict:** Individuals within the community may feel emotionally torn due to the tension between the selective use of scripture verses and their religious beliefs. This conflict can lead to emotional instability and anxiety.

3. **Manipulation of Faith:** The community can experience a sense of manipulation, where they are steered in a direction that serves the leader's interests rather than the sincere search for spiritual truth. This manipulation can have a profound impact on the profession of faith.

4. **Confusion about Truth:** Cherry-picking can cause confusion about the true meaning of religious teachings. Community members may question whether the leader understands the true importance of scripture or whether religious practice is grounded in true spirituality.

Examples of Cherry-Picking:

1. **Prosperity Gospel:** A leader who preaches a prosperity gospel can selectively overuse scripture verses that support the idea of wealth and health while ignoring the verses warning against greed for money and materialism.
2. **Suppression of Criticism:** A leader who opposes criticism may choose scripture verses that support the idea of absolute obedience to the leader while ignoring the texts that encourage asking and questioning.
3. **Exclusive Salvation:** A leader with a complete view of salvation may choose texts supporting the idea of limited and exclusive salvation while ignoring texts about grace and religious freedom.

Metaphors and Allegories in Depth:

Another tactic of a narcissistic leader is the distortion of symbolic texts, such as metaphors and allegories, to create a narrative that serves his interests. This technique draws on the richness of figurative language to promote a specific interpretation, often at the expense of the text's original intent.

Psychological Impact of Distortion of Symbolic Texts:

1. **Confusion and uncertainty:** Using symbolic language can lead to confusion and tension within the community. Individuals may struggle to understand the message's true meaning.
2. **Control of Interpretation:** A leader may use symbolic texts to gain control over the interpretation of religious doctrines. This control allows him to steer the community in a specific direction and advance his agenda.
3. **Changing Truth:** The manipulation of symbolic texts can change the community's perception of truth. It can change

a community's relationship with the religious teachings and create a new reality according to the leader's interpretation.

Examples of Distortion of Symbolic Texts:

1. **Apocalyptic Interpretation:** A leader can distort an apocalyptic allegory to create a sphere of fear and panic within the community to ensure control and obedience.
2. **Suppression of Dissensibility:** Symbolic texts can suppress dissension and criticism by emphasizing the idea of divine punishment for those who stand up against the leader.
3. **Creating a Utopia:** A leader can use a utopian allegory to ensure the community's loyalty and promote complete obedience to his authority.

Concluding Thoughts:
The distortion of the Word by the selective use of scriptures and the manipulation of symbolic texts by a narcissistic leader has a profound psychological impact on a community. This impact includes confusion, uncertainty, and a changed perception of truth. The community may experience a sense of dependence and develop an underlying dysfunction that can further lead to emotional conflict and faith disruption. Awareness of these dangers is critical to preserve a community's psychological well-being and maintain a healthy interaction with religious teachings.

Chapter 4 - How can narcissistic sect leaders urge followers about essential Christian doctrines?

Gaslighting is a form of psychological manipulation that causes a person to doubt their own perception, memory, or judgment. Narcissistic leaders may use gaslighting to control, manipulate, or exploit their followers, especially regarding Christian doctrine.

Here are 10 possible ways narcissistic leaders can gas their followers over Christian doctrine:

- They may deny or distort the historical facts or evidence that support Christianity's truth, such as the resurrection of Jesus, the reliability of the Bible, or the fulfillment of prophecies.

- They can distort or misuse Scripture to justify their actions, beliefs, or agendas and condemn or criticize those who disagree. They can take verses out of context, ignore the original meaning or intent, or apply them selectively or inconsistently.

- They may establish or impose rules, regulations, or rituals based not on Scripture but on their preferences, traditions, or opinions. They may demand that their followers abide by these rules, regulations, or rituals and accuse them of disobeying, rebellious, or unfaithful if they do not.

- They may isolate or alienate their followers from their family, friends, or other sources of support, information, or influence. They may claim that these people are worldly, sinful, or hostile to the leader or the group, and their followers should avoid or cut off contact with them. They may also discourage or prohibit their followers from seeking or receiving help or advice from anyone outside the leader or the group, such as pastors, counselors, or experts.

- They may instill fear, guilt, or shame in their followers and use it to manipulate their emotions, thoughts, or behaviors. They may threaten their followers with divine judgment, punishment, or rejection if they do not obey, comply, or conform to the leader or the group. They may also blame their followers for their problems, failures, sins, or the leader or group's problems, failures, or immorality. They may also make their followers feel unworthy, inadequate, or flawed and make them dependent on the leader or the group for ratification, approval, or acceptance.

- They may lie, deceive, or withhold information from their followers, presenting themselves as the sole or ultimate source of truth, knowledge, or wisdom. They may claim to have a unique insight, understanding, or connection to God that their followers do not have and that their followers should not question, challenge, or verify anything they say or do. They may also hide, cover up, deny their mistakes, flaws, or sins, or blame them on others. This is absolutely contrary to how the Apostle Paul's message was scrutinized by the Bereans, which was, in fact, something Paul encouraged.

- They may exploit or abuse their followers physically, emotionally, sexually, or spiritually and justify or rationalize their actions using Scripture, doctrine, or belief. They may claim they have a divine right, mandate, or permission to do what they do and that their followers must submit, obey, or consent. They may also claim that their actions are for their followers' benefit, growth, or salvation and that their followers should be grateful, loyal, or faithful to them.

- They may create or promote a culture of secrecy, loyalty, or conformity among their followers, discouraging or suppressing discord, diversity, or individuality. They may claim a special mission, vision, or purpose from God that their followers should support, follow, or join. They may also claim to be the only genuine, authentic, or faithful representation of Christianity and that their followers should not associate or cooperate with any other Christians, churches, or organizations.

- They may compare or contrast themselves or their group with other Christians, churches, or organizations and portray themselves or their group as superior, better, or more favored by God. They may claim to have a higher standard, quality, or level of spirituality, morality, or service than others and that their followers should be proud, confident, or content with them. They may also criticize, ridicule, or slander other Christians, churches, or organizations, portraying them as inferior, worse, or less favored by God.
- They can manipulate or influence their followers' perception of reality, making them doubt their senses, experiences, or intuition. They may claim that what their followers see, hear, feel, or remember is not valid, accurate, or trustworthy and that their followers should not trust them. They may also claim that what they say, do, or show is the true, accurate, or reliable reality and that their followers should trust them.

These are some of the ways narcissistic leaders can gass their followers over Christian doctrine. Still, there may be others not mentioned.

Chapter 5 - How would a narcissistic church leader misuses Mal 3:9-11 to raise more money for himself or his ministry?

1. Focus on the "complete obedience" in Malachi 3:9:

Narcissistic church leaders may use the first few verses of Malachi 3 to emphasize the idea of perfect obedience. They could argue that if the followers do not faithfully tithe and sacrifice to God, they disobey God and cannot experience the full blessing of God. This approach puts the leader in a position where he represents divine authority and holds the key to the full blessing of God.

He can argue that the compliance of followers is expressed through faithful financial contributions, especially in the form of tithes and sacrifices. This approach is a powerful control tool in which the leader sees himself as the authority on divine approval and blessings.

The leader may emphasize that the Bible clearly provides financial contributions as a sign of loyalty to God. According to his interpretation of Malagai 3:9, obedience to his financial guidelines is tantamount to obedience to God. This manipulative interpretation makes it difficult for followers to question the leader's authority without questioning their faith in God at the same time.

This focus on "complete obedience" strengthened the narcissistic leader's grip on the followers, as they constantly feared the possibility of divine disapproval due to failure to make financial contributions. This creates a culture of dependency and blind obedience, in which individuals must set aside their own judgments and values to support the leader's financial agenda.

2. Terror image of cursing in Malachi 3:9-11:

The leader can use the verses of Malachi 3 to leave a terror image of a curse hanging over the followers if they do not fully comply with the tithes and sacrifices. By emphasizing the threat of a curse, the leader manipulates the emotional state of the followers and makes them fearful about the possible negative consequences of not making financial contributions.

This leader deliberately takes advantage of the threat of cursing to create an atmosphere of fear and uncertainty in the community. He may make the followers feel that failing to make loyal and adequate financial contributions leads to an inevitable divine punishment.

These tactics indicate the narcissistic leader's willingness to use emotional manipulation to further his financial agenda. By emphasizing the threat of a curse, he puts followers in a vulnerable position, terrified about the possibility of negative consequences if they fail to meet his financial demands.

This manipulative approach puts the leader in the position of savior, according to which followers see their financial commitment to him as a way to protect themselves from the impending divine punishment.

Thus, the narcissistic leader uses the threat of cursing in Malagai 3:9-11 to create a climate of fear and dependence, with which he enforces financial contributions and strengthens his own power and control. This manipulative strategy illustrates the leader's willingness to abuse religious beliefs to advance his own agenda and force followers to make financial contributions for fear of divine disapproval.

3. Distortion of "opening windows of heaven" in Mal 3:10:

Narcissistic leaders can use the image of "opening the windows of heaven" as a picture of unlocking financial wealth and prosperity. They may interpret this as a divine promise that if followers give lavishly, God will uniquely pour out financial blessings upon them. This distortion of the text promotes the idea that financial contributions are directly linked to the personal prosperity of the followers.

The narcissistic leader uses the Bible to establish a philosophy of personal wealth, in which he presents himself as the key to divine blessings and financial wealth.

The leader may argue that obeying his financial guidelines opens the "windows of heaven," which are seen as a divine source of economic prosperity. He can use this interpretation to convince followers that the degree of their financial contributions is directly tied to the amount of blessings they receive from God.

This tactic reinforces the narcissistic leader's role as the intermediary between God and the followers. He offers them a false promise of divine blessings in exchange for obedience to his financial demands.

This approach can create a climate of financial pressure in which followers feel compelled to give more in hopes of an extraordinary financial reward.

It serves as an effective tactic to fill the leader's own pocket. At the same time, followers view their financial sacrifices as a direct investment in their prosperity and divine blessings.

4. Personal reward for financial contributions:

Narcissistic leaders can promote the idea that those who give more will be a particular favorite of God. They can create a hierarchy of financial contributions and make promises of personal divine protection, health, and wealth for those who give. This manipulative tactic allows the leader to create a culture of competition between followers to give more, thus filling his own pocket.

This leader creates a hierarchy of financial contributions and provides promises of personal divine favor for those who give more. By promoting a systematic arrangement of monetary donations, the leader sets up an environment of competition among followers, in which they compete for higher levels of divine favor and protection.

This manipulative strategy uses a reward system to motivate followers to sacrifice more financially. The leader may suggest that their financial contributions are directly tied to the degree of personal divine blessings and prosperity they will experience. These promises of personal favor can range from health and wellness to an elevated spiritual status within the community.

The narcissistic leader becomes the decisive mediator of this reward system, with which he expands his power and influence. This approach creates a climate in which followers make financial contributions and see them as a way to win the leader's favor and receive personally beneficial treatment.

This tactic highlights the narcissistic leader's ability to cultivate not only financial but also emotional and spiritual dependency among followers. By linking the promise of personal divine blessings to financial contributions, the leader manipulates followers' motivations and creates a dynamic in which obedience to his financial agenda is seen as a direct path to personal prosperity and divine favor.

5. Self-glorification by the "treasure house of the church":

Narcissistic leaders may use the image of the "treasure house of the church" to emphasize their grandeur. They can promote the idea that the church's wealth reflects the divine blessing on their leadership and that followers participate in this divine wealth through their financial contributions. This approach serves as a means for the leader to glorify himself by linking his personal success to the financial contributions of the followers.

This leader manipulates the Bible verse Malagai 3:9-11 by reversing the idea of a wealthy church into an instrument of self-glorification.

By presenting the church's wealth as an indicator of divine blessing, the leader creates a climate in which followers directly associate the church's wealth with his own divine mediation and leadership. This approach elevates the leader to an exalted status, where his success and wealth are seen as a sign of his unique bond with God.

The leader can use it to cultivate a culture of admiration and idolatry, in which followers see him as the controller of the divine treasure house. This dynamic allows him to soothe his ego by linking the church's wealth to his success and ruling authority. This makes it difficult for followers to question his leadership without doubting the church's supposed divine blessing and protection at the same time.

This tactic demonstrates the narcissistic leader's willingness to abuse religious symbols and institutions to promote his own grandeur. Using the image of the "treasure house of the church," the leader creates a culture in which his own prosperity is seen as a direct reflection of divine approval, placing him in a position of unassailable leadership.

6. Abuse of the "and I will stop the forager for you" in Malachi 3:11:

The leader can abuse the verses about "I will stop the forager for you" by using them out of context to emphasize the idea of financial protection from any form of loss or bad financial matters. This tactic motivates followers to give more as a form of self-protection from financial trouble.

This leader may deliberately interpret this Bible verse as a promise of divine care and protection from financial hardship, provided that followers remain true to his financial guidelines.

Using this promise of protection as a motivation, the leader can convince followers to sacrifice more financially, arguing that obeying his financial guidelines ensures a direct path to financial stability and security. This manipulative tactic creates a climate in which followers see their financial contributions as assurance against any economic challenges.

The leader uses the phrase "and I will stop the forager for you" to emphasize the idea of a protective divine hand, which is available only through obedience to his financial agenda. This approach can force followers to see their financial sacrifices as necessary to ensure divine protection and avoid any doubt or opposition for fear of the potential consequences.

This tactic serves to strengthen the narcissistic leader's power through the semblance of divine protection and care linked to financial obedience. This creates an environment in which followers tend to give more, not only as a form of compliance but also as a strategy to protect themselves from financial insecurity. This manipulative approach underscores the leader's willingness to distort religious principles to advance his power, control, and financial gain agenda.

7. Threat of deprivation without financial contributions:

Narcissistic leaders may threaten that followers will be subjected to financial hardship if they do not tithe faithfully. This tactic puts followers in a position where they are terrified about the possibility of economic disaster due to insufficient contributions.

This leader may emphasize that failing to faithfully tithe and sacrifice results in financial hardship and a lack of divine blessings. This manipulative tactic makes followers vulnerable and terrified about the possibility of economic disaster due to insufficient contributions.

Using the threat of deprivation, the leader creates a climate of fear and dependence, in which followers not only make their financial contributions but also do so out of fear of the potential negative consequences of disobedience. This approach serves as an effective tactic to manipulate followers into staying true to its financial guidelines even in the absence of clear evidence of divine blessings.

The leader uses this threat of deprivation to cultivate an atmosphere of desperation, in which followers see their financial contributions as a form of self-preservation against potentially harmful outcomes. This tactic puts the leader in a position where he has control over not only the financial flows within the church but also the emotional state of followers, who are terrified by the possible consequences of non-faithful financial contributions.

This manipulative approach illustrates the narcissistic leader's willingness to introduce fear and deprivation as tactics to force followers to meet his financial demands. By emphasizing the deprivation resulting from disobedience, the leader establishes a climate in which followers are willing to give more to evade possible negative consequences.

8. Conditioning divine approval on financial contributions:

The leader can emphasize the imaginary connection between financial contributions and divine approval. He can promote the idea that those who experience wealth owe it to their faithful tithes. In contrast, those who struggle with finances do not fully experience the divine blessing. This approach conditioned followers to follow the leader's guidelines to secure divine approval.

This leader manipulates the Bible verse Malagai 3:9-11 by emphasizing the imaginary relationship between financial contributions and divine approval. He may claim that those who experience wealth and prosperity owe it to their faithful fulfillment of financial obligations. At the same time, those who struggle with finances do not receive the full divine blessings.

This manipulative approach conditioned followers to link their worth and divine blessing directly to their financial contributions. The leader serves as the arbitrator of this divine approval, and his position is considered the key to the full grace of God. This conditioning of support and blessing creates a culture in which followers not only make financial contributions but do so as a way to secure their own divine acceptance.

This tactic serves as a way for the narcissistic leader to strengthen his influence by convincing followers that they deserve financial and divine approval through obedience to his financial agenda. The leader's position as mediator of divine grace gives him extraordinary control and influence because followers are willing to make financial sacrifices as a direct path to divine blessings and approval.

9. Promotion of a "spiritual investment" philosophy:

Narcissistic leaders may see financial contributions as an investment in the kingdom of God. They can argue that those who give in ample will receive a high return on their "spiritual investment." This approach promotes a view of financial contributions as a divine investment influencing individuals' spiritual progress.

This leader can see financial contributions as an investment in the kingdom of God, where the degree of contributions is directly linked to the expectation of a high return on this spiritual investment.

The leader may argue that those who give lavishly will be a particular favorite of God and will experience a higher level of spiritual blessings and prosperity. This manipulative approach uses the idea of a spiritual investment to convince followers that financial contributions are not just a material sacrifice but an opportunity to ensure a high return on their spiritual investment.

The leader creates a culture in which followers not only make their financial contributions but also do so with a view to the promise of increased spiritual well-being and closer to God. This tactic strengthens the narcissistic leader's grip on the followers because they are willing to give more not only as a form of obedience but as a strategy for achieving a higher spiritual status.

Promoting a "spiritual investment" philosophy leads followers to believe that the leader's guidelines have a financial impact and a direct impact on their spiritual destiny. This manipulative approach creates a climate in which followers are willing to give lavishly in hopes of receiving an extraordinary spiritual reward, and it affirms the narcissistic leader's position as the mediator of this spiritual investment strategy.

10. Decoupling self-enrichment from reality:

Narcissistic leaders may disconnect financial contributions from personal self-enrichment by arguing that the money is only used for spreading the gospel and expanding the church. This tactic allows the leader to accumulate wealth without guilt. At the same time, followers become convinced that their contributions are only for spiritual purposes.

This leader may promote the idea that financial contributions are destined solely for the spread of the gospel and the church's expansion and that any wealth accumulated is only a reflection of the divine blessing on his leadership.

Through this disconnection of self-enrichment from reality, the leader creates a narrative in which his wealth is seen not as a direct result of financial contributions but as a natural result of his divine authority and blessing. This manipulative approach allows the leader to accumulate wealth without guilt while persuading followers that their financial contributions are used only for the divine mission of the church.

This tactic serves as a strategy to neutralize any doubts or criticism of followers since the leader dismisses himself from the suspicion of self-enrichment. It also reinforces the narcissistic leader's image as a selfless and devoted servant of God while simultaneously accumulating his personal wealth and power behind the scenes.

The disengagement of self-enrichment from reality is an ingenious manipulative strategy because it allows the leader to accumulate wealth without making the followers doubt his motives or moral integrity. This tactic indicates the narcissistic leader's ability to manage the perceptions of the community and advance his own interests without arousing the semblance of selfishness.

Chapter 6: The Psychology of Manipulation

Gaslighting Techniques: How the leader sows doubt, denies reality, and applies emotional manipulation.

The Growing Dependency: How Followers Are Made Dependent Through Manipulation of Emotions and Perceptions.

The Psychology of Manipulation - Gaslighting in Religious Leadership

Introduction:

Gaslighting, a subtle but destructive form of emotional manipulation, is a frequent tactic of narcissistic leaders to take control of their community.

This chapter examines the psychological impact of gaslighting in religious leadership, including its manifestations, its effects on individuals within the community, and the structural dynamics that make gaslighting possible.

Manifestations of Gaslighting in Religious Leadership:

Gaslighting in the context of religious leadership often takes several forms, and it is crucial to understand its subtle but destructive manifestations.

1. Doubts Sown about Own Judgment:

A narcissistic leader may deliberately sow doubt about the community's own judgment and experiences. This tactic can be highly destructive because it undermines the individual's self-confidence and makes them dependent on the leader's views.

2. Denial of Reality:

The leader can deny or distort reality to advance his own narrative. If community members experience reality differently from what the leader presents, they may be accused of misunderstanding or deception.

3. Debt shift:

Gaslighting often includes debt shifting, where the leader shifts the blame from adverse outcomes to community/church members. This tactic can cause individuals to question their own self-worth.

4. Isolation:

Community members who may experience doubts may be isolated from others to minimize the impact of their questions and concerns. This isolation creates a climate in which individuals lose judgment on important issues.

5. Dishonest Award of Alleged Revelations:

Gaslighters may award themselves as the only recipients of special revelations or insight, which can pressure the community's members to worship and obey the leader.

The Psychological Consequences of Gaslighting:

Gaslighting has a range of psychological severe consequences for individuals within a community. These consequences are often subtle and riddled with emotional damage.

1. Emotional Instability:

Gasing can lead to severe emotional instability, where individuals feel persistently insecure about their own perceptions and judgments. This instability can have an impact on the overall emotional well-being of the community.

2. Loss of Self-Confidence:

Individuals who are constantly exposed to doubts may lose their self-confidence. This loss of self-confidence can negatively affect self-esteem and the ability to make healthy decisions.

3. Increased Anxiety and Depression:

Gaslighting is often linked to an increased level of anxiety and depression within a community. Individuals may be in a perpetual state of uncertainty and fear of the consequences of their actions and judgments.

4. Decline in Self-Reliance:

The constant manipulation of reality can lead to a decrease in self-reliance. Community members may be hypocritical about thinking and taking action independently for fear of the negative consequences of their judgments.

5. *Loss of Community Connection:*

Gaslighting can undermine the community's interconnectedness and trust. Individuals may become distrustful of each other because of the uncertainty created by gaslighting.

Structural Dynamics That Make Gaslighting Possible:

Gaslighting often thrives in a specific structural context within the community. This dynamic contributes to the persistence of gaslighting by the leader.

1. Hierarchical Structure:

A hierarchical structure, in which the leader has excessive power without adequate oversight, creates a climate where gaslighting can occur unhindered.

2. Lack of Transparency:

The absence of transparency and open communication in the leadership creates a space where gaslighting can thrive. Flawed information can catalyze confusion and manipulation.

3. Control over Information:

Gaslighting is often effective if the leader controls the information presented to the community. The manipulation of information and the restriction of access to alternative views contribute to the persistence of gaslighting.

4. Peer Pressure and Affirmation:

Peer pressure and the quest for affirmation within the community create a climate in which individuals do not feel free to stand against the gaslighting. Affirming the leader's views becomes a priority, even at the expense of one's judgment.

5. Large degree of dependency:

A large degree of dependence on the leader and a strong emotional connection with the community can increase the effectiveness of gaslighting. Individuals feel more constrained to stand up to the leader for fear of rejection or isolation.

How narcissistic leaders abuse gaslighting:
Promotes Infallibility:

Narcissistic leaders often create an image of untouchability and divine infallibility. These leaders can present themselves as the only source of religious knowledge and discourage doubt or criticism. Followers may learn that to question the leader is to rebel against God Himself. This dynamic makes it difficult for followers to challenge the leader's authority, even when there are clear signs of abuse or malpractice.

Doubting own observation:

Gaslighting often includes individuals beginning to doubt their own observation if it is inconsistent with the leader's narrative. The leader may subtly suggest that the followers are not sufficiently spiritually enlightened to see the truth. This uncertainty encourages dependence because followers then no longer consider themselves trustworthy.

Guilt and shame:

Narcissistic leaders can use guilt to exert control. Criticism of the leader or questioning can be presented as blasphemy or rebellion. The leader can portray themselves as the only path to salvation; any deviation from this path can be followed by intense spiritual guilt and shame, urging followers to remain obedient.

Control over information:

The leader can selectively provide information and suppress alternative views by exercising control over information. It reinforces the leader's authority as the sole interpreter of divine truth while limiting followers to an aside perspective. This information isolation contributes to the reduction of critical thinking and makes followers more susceptible to manipulation.

Encourages Isolation:

Narcissistic leaders may encourage followers to associate only with fellow sect members and avoid outsiders. This isolation reinforces groupthink and makes it difficult for individuals to gain alternative perspectives. The group becomes a priJane source of social identity, strengthening the leader's influence.

Variable reality creates:

Narcissistic leaders can deliberately change doctrines and rules to create a sphere of constant uncertainty. This changeable reality makes it harder for followers to firmly grasp the truth. When religious beliefs constantly change, individuals depend on the leader to provide guidelines and direction. This dependence strengthens the leader's influence and control over followers' minds.

Reducing self-confidence:

Criticism of the leader or his teaching can be interpreted as a lack of faith or spiritual weakness. The leader can lead followers to believe that any doubt of the doctrine can cause the loss of God's favor. This tactic reduces the confidence of individuals to use their own judgment, whereby they are more likely to blindly follow the leader.

Making Love Conditional:

Narcissistic leaders may promote a view that God's love is available only to those perfectly obedient to the leader's precepts. This conditional love creates a climate where followers must put aside their needs and longings to receive divine approval. The leader uses love as an instrument of control and manipulation.

Intimidation and threats:

To ensure obedience, the leader may threaten with divine wrath or eternal punishment those who do not comply with his orders. This tactic introduces a sphere of fear into the community and discourages any form of opposition. Followers fear not only the leader himself but also the supposed divine consequences of disobedience.

Personal Attacks and Humiliation:

Critics of dissident members may be exposed to personal attacks and demeaning tactics. This strategy serves to deter other members from expressing their misgivings. It reinforces a climate in which dissension is seen as personal betrayal. The leader manipulates the emotional vulnerability of individuals to keep them in a position of submission.

1. **Selective Interpretation:** Narcissistic leaders may selectively interpret Christian doctrine and emphasize parts consistent with their agenda while rejecting or distorting others to fit their narrative.

2. **Claim to Exclusive Revelation:** Gaslighting leaders may claim exclusive insights or revelations about Christian doctrine, discouraging followers from questioning or seeking alternative interpretations.

3. **Manipulating Scripture:** Narcissistic sect leaders can manipulate biblical passages, take them out of context, or change their meaning to support their teachings and control the interpretation of Christian doctrine.

4. **Doubts about traditional beliefs:** Gaslighters may cast doubt on established Christian beliefs, question the validity of generally accepted doctrines, and present their interpretations as superior or more enlightening.

5. **Creating a Cult of Personality:** Narcissistic leaders can interweave their own persona with Christian doctrine and convince followers that their teachings are inseparable from the core tenets of the faith.

6. **Discouraging Independent Study:** Gaslighting leaders may prevent followers from independently studying the Bible or consulting alternative sources, furthering dependence on the leader's interpretation of Christian doctrine.

7. **Fear-Based Manipulation:** Narcissistic sect leaders can instill fear by claiming that deviating from their interpretation of Christian doctrine will lead to dire consequences and manipulate followers into complying.

8. **Distorting Grace and Forgiveness:** Gaslighters can manipulate the concepts of mercy and forgiveness and selectively use them to excuse their actions while applying harsh judgment to followers who question their teachings.

9. **Isolating Dissidents:** Narcissistic leaders can isolate and demonize those who question or challenge their interpretation of Christian doctrine, creating an environment where dissent is seen as a threat to faith. This isolation may also be applied to those who have left the ministry in which the narcissist operates. Congregants may also be instructed not to have contact, or entertain contact with the one who left. Even previously elevated staff, complimented on the anointing on their lives, may be neglected upon leaving the ministry.

10. **Fostering a Sense of Specialness:** Gaslighting leaders can convince followers that their sect has exclusive and superior insights into Christian doctrine, fostering a sense of elitism that discourages critical examination of their teachings. The narcissist may also (in hindsight) proclaim foreknowledge – although it was never shared with anyone.

Chapter 7 - The Jezebel Spirit and Narcissism: A Comparison of Biblical Images and Psychological Concepts – with reference to DSM-5.

Introduction:

The concept of the "Jezebel spirit" in a religious context often has affinities with the psychological concept of narcissism. These concepts have their origins in the Bible, specifically in the stories of Queen Jezebel.

This chapter will attempt to explore the similarities and differences between these biblical images and the psychological concept of narcissism while making references to relevant scriptures.

1. Jezebel in the Bible: A Profile:

Jezebel, described in the Old Testament, was a queen of Israel, married to King Ahab. Her rule was marked by religious apostasy and manipulation. One of the most prominent Bible passages that tells Jezebel's story is 1 Kings 16:29-34 and 1 Kings 18:1-4.

1.1 Religious Worship:

- Jezebel promotes the worship of the god Baal, an idol inconsistent with the worship of the only true God, YHWH. This aspect of her character illustrates religious apostasy and a rejection of a higher authority.

1.2 Manipulation and cruelty:

- In 1 Kings 21:5-16, we see Jezebel's manipulation to obtain a vinyard for Ahab through false testimony and the unlawful execution of Naboth, the owner of the vinyard. From this arises a willingness to manipulate and a lack of moral consideration.

2. Narcissism as a Psychological Concept:

Narcissism is a psychological condition characterized by excessive self-importance, a lack of empathy, and a strong desire for recognition and admiration. The Diagnostic and Statistical Manual of Mental Health Conditions (DSM-5) identifies Narcissistic Personality Disorder (NPV) as a clinical condition.

2.1 Characteristics of Narcissism:

- The characteristics of NPV include a strong need for admiration, a lack of empathy, explicit fantasies of unprecedented success, a sense of self-importance, and a tendency to use people for personal gain.

Diagnosis of Narcissistic Personality Disorder:

To be diagnosed with NPV, according to the DSM-5, an individual must meet a specific set of criteria. These criteria include a pattern of behaviors that began in early adulthood, are persistent over a long period, and manifest in various situations.

3. Criticism and Controversy:

It is important to note that the diagnosis of personality disorders, including NPV, is not without controversy. Some critics claim that the criteria for personality disorders are sometimes vague and that there can be an overlap between several conditions. Others emphasize the subjective nature of the diagnosis process.

4. Treatment and Approaches:

The treatment of NPV may be inclusive, but it often includes psychotherapy. Therapy may focus on developing empathy, dealing with criticism, and promoting healthy interpersonal relationships. There isn't a specific medication for NPV. Still, medication can be used to treat associated symptoms, such as depression or anxiety.

Concluding Thoughts:

The Diagnostic and Statistical Manual of Mental Health Conditions (DSM-5) identification of Narcissistic Personality Disorder as a clinical condition highlights the serious nature of this pattern of behavior and emotional functioning. While the manual is helpful for healthcare professionals, it is crucial to apply care and empathy when working with individuals with NPV because treatment is often a complex and lengthy process.

Diagnostic and Statistical Manual of Mental Health Conditions (DSM-5)

The **Diagnostic and Statistical Manual of Mental Health Conditions (DSM-5)** is an essential resource for healthcare professionals to diagnose and classify psychiatric conditions. This manual, created by the American Psychiatric Association, describes a wide variety of psychiatric conditions, including personality disorders.

One of the personality disorders described is **Narcissistic Personality Disorder (NPV)**. This condition focuses on excessive selfishness, a lack of empathy for others, and an intense search for admiration and recognition.

Let's explore this statement in more depth:

1. Narcissistic Personality Disorder (NPV) in the DSM-5:

The DSM-5 identifies NPV as a distinct personality disorder characterized by a pattern of excessive selfishness, a need for admiration, and a lack of empathy. These patterns of behaviors and attitudes often cause difficulties in personal relationships, work settings, and other areas of life.

2. Core characteristics of Narcissistic Personality Disorder:

The DSM-5 identifies specific factors typically found in individuals with NPV:

2.1 Excessive self-worthiness:

- Individuals with NPV often have an excess of self-worth and a conviction of their own uniqueness and importance. They may feel that they can only be understood by others like them.

2.2 Lack of Empathy:

- A distinct lack of empathy towards the needs and emotions of others is a hallmark of NPV. This lack of empathy can lead to unsuitable interpersonal interactions.

2.3 Pursuit of Admiration:

- An intense need for admiration from others is another feature. Individuals with NPV constantly seek recognition and praise to maintain their self-worth.

2.4 Relationship problems:

- NPV often causes problems in personal relationships because the individual exploits people to achieve personal goals and has difficulty entering into a real, reciprocal relationship.

2.5 Sensitive to Criticism:

- People with NPV are often susceptible to criticism. They can react defensively when they are not receiving the admiration they desire.

3.2 Overlaps with Jezebel:

- There are clear overlaps between the biblical images of Jezebel and the characteristics of narcissism. The manipulation, religious apostasy, and an unlimited desire for control and power are core aspects of both the biblical figures and the psychological concept.

4. Similarities between the Jezebel spirit and Narcissism:
4.1 Manipulation:

- Jezebel exhibits a strong tendency toward manipulation to benefit themselves. This manipulation includes false testimony, wrongful executions, and the use of power structures to control others.

4.2 Lack of Empathy:

- The religious and social acts of Jezebel illustrate a considerable lack of empathy towards the suffering of others. This lack of empathy is a crucial feature of narcissism.

4.3 Desire for Control:

- Jezebel desired intensive control over her environment, including the religious and political servants. This desire for power goes hand in hand with pursuing self-importance and self-glorification.

5. Differences and subtle nuances:
5.1 Religious context:

- A significant difference is the pronounced religious context in which the Jezebel spirit appears. This image emphasizes the manipulation of religious power structures for personal gain, while narcissism is often a broader psychological concept.

5.2 Biblical Inference:

- The term "Jezebel spirit" is derived from a biblical figure, while the word "narcissism" is a psychological label. These inferences contribute to each concept's unique context and meaning.

6. The Cautionary Element of Biblical Imagery:

The biblical images of Jezebel serve as cautionary examples of the devastating effects of religious manipulation, cruelty, and an obsession with personal power and control. These biblical narratives provide an ethical framework for recognizing the dangers of selfish and manipulative behavior within a religious context.

Concluding Thoughts:

The similarities between the Jezebel spirit and the psychological concept of narcissism lie in the manipulation, lack of empathy, and desire for power and control. These concepts, each with its unique context, provide insight into the potential dangers of a selfish approach to management and influence. While the biblical imagery serves as a moral warning, the psychological concept of narcissism provides a framework for understanding these patterns of behavior within a broader psychological context.

Chapter 8: Disruption of Traditional Teachings

Rejecting Traditional Doctrines: How the Leader Can Deform Basic Doctrines to Serve His Own Agenda.

Exclusive Revelations: The claim that the leader receives exclusive revelations and how they affect the faith community.

Introduction:

Moral double standards, applying different ethical criteria to various individuals or groups, are highly disruptive aspects of religious leadership.

This chapter examines the psychological and social impact of moral double standards within a community, including their manifestations, their effects on individuals, and the structural dynamics that maintain them.

Manifestations of Moral Double Standards in Religious Leadership:

Moral double standards in religious leadership often take subtle but insidious forms. These manifestations contribute to a climate in which the leader applies an unequal standard of ethical behavior.

1. Selective Application of Sin:

A narcissistic leader may have a selective approach to sin acceptance, in which specific individuals' sins are forgiven. In contrast, others' sins are judged with rigor. This unequal handling of sin creates a climate of injustice within the community.

2. Prejudice of Certain Individuals:

Moral double standards often manifest as favoritism of specific individuals within the community. The leader may have favorites that are not subjected to the same ethical standards as others.

3. Restriction of Freedom of Expression:

Individuals within the community may be restricted in their freedom of expression if their opinions or views are inconsistent with the leader's views. This restriction contributes to a climate of self-censorship and conformism.

4. Distortion of Doctrines:

Moral double standards may also be visible in distorting religious doctrines to conform to the leader's agenda. Certain ethical principles can be emphasized or distorted to justify a specific outcome.

5. Exclusivity and Discrimination:

The leader may promote an exclusive view of morality, leading to discrimination of specific individuals within the community. This discrimination may be based on race, gender, sexual orientation, or other personal characteristics.

The Psychological Consequences of Moral Double Standards:

The application of moral double standards in religious leadership has a far-reaching impact on the psychological well-being of individuals within the community.

1. Loss of Self-Respect:

Individuals subject to unjust moral judgments may experience a loss of self-respect. This can harm self-esteem and self-confidence.

2. Moral Confusion:

The unequal application of moral measures can lead to moral confusion within the community. Individuals may struggle to develop a stable, ethical framework due to the conflict between the leader's views and their moral beliefs.

3. Distrust of Authority:

Moral double standards can lead to distrust of the leader's authority and the community's broader institutions. This distrust can cause further social disruption.

4. Decline in Community Affiliation:

The application of moral double standards can lead to a decrease in the interrelationship within the community. Individuals may find themselves in a climate of social distancing and isolation.

5. Inner Conflict and Crisis of Conscience:

Community members may experience inner conflict between their own moral convictions and the imposed moral benchmarks of the leader. This internal conflict can lead to a crisis of conscience and emotional disruption.

Structural Dynamics Maintaining Moral Double Standards:

The persistence of moral double standards in religious leadership is often linked to specific structural dynamics within the community.

1. Hierarchical Structure:

A hierarchical structure in which the leader possesses excessive power contributes to the persistence of moral double standards. This power structure allows the leader to favor specific individuals while oppressing others.

2. Lack of Accountability:

The absence of an effective accountability system allows the leader to apply unchecked moral double standards. A lack of transparency and independent oversight makes it difficult for individuals to stand up against unfair practices.

3. Control over Information and Communication:

The leader's control over information and communication contributes to maintaining moral double standards. Limited access to information may preclude individuals from obtaining a complete picture of the situation.

4. Peer Pressure and Affirmation:

Peer pressure and the quest for confirmation can deter individuals from standing up against moral double standards. The fear of ostracization or seclusion can hinder individuals from having their voices heard.

5. Manipulation of Doctrines:

The manipulation of religious doctrines to adapt to the leader's agenda reinforces the persistence of moral double standards. The leader may emphasize or distort certain principles to justify his own views.

Concluding Thoughts:

Moral double standards in religious leadership are a disruptive force that threatens the psychological well-being of a community. This creates a climate of injustice, moral confusion, and social dislocation. The awareness of these manifestations, their effects, and the structural dynamics that maintain them are essential to fostering a healthy and ethical environment within a community.

Chapter 9: The Encounters of the Defeated

Those who leave the ministry and control of a narcissistic leader are often isolated. This isolation may be ring-fencing the individual so that the individual may not operate in a similar field of ministry because of a fear of exposure.

Those left behind under the control of the narcissist will also be instructed not to have anything to do with the one who left. This is mainly done to protect the narcissist's failure or limitation.

In this Chapter, we will be looking at various reasons why narcissists ring fence those leaving the ministry.

Herewith are 10 reasons why people left behind are instructed to ignore others who leave a sect or church led by a narcissistic leader.

1. **Control and Power:** Narcissistic leaders thrive on control. Discouraging recognition of departures ensures that the leader remains the priJane authority figure, controls the narrative, and prevents alternative viewpoints.

2. **Image preservation:** Ignoring deviations is a strategy for maintaining a positive public image. Leaders may fear that recognizing anomalies could lead to negative publicity, damaging the sect or church's reputation and the perceived success of the leader.

3. **Isolation Tactics:** By isolating former members, the leader maintains a barrier against the possible spread of dissenting opinions. This tactic precludes a collective understanding of shared negative experiences, reinforcing that leaving is an isolated and wrong choice.

4. **Fear of Contagion:** There is a fear that recognizing those who leave may expose current members to critical perspectives, leading to doubts about the legitimacy of the sect or church.

Leaders want to protect followers from any information that might challenge their commitment.

5. **Avoid doubt:** Recognition of anomalies may prompt current members to question the leader's decisions or the sect or church's principles. By ignoring those who leave, the leader seeks to create an environment where doubt is suppressed, with a façade of unwavering conviction.

6. **Maintaining Allegiance:** Ignoring defections reinforces a sense of loyalty among remaining members. The leader strategically defines those who leave as disloyal or misguided and fosters a stronger bond between those who stay by creating an "us versus them" mentality. Those leaving are often called "not following the vision" anymore.

7. **Suppression of Dissent:** Recognizing deviations can trigger open conversations about discontent or concerns within the sect or church. Ignoring those who leave, the leader suppresses internal discord and maintains a façade of unity and commitment.

8. **Denial of Problems:** Leaders can be invested in denying the existence of problems within the sect or church. By ignoring deviations, they can downplay any issues, perpetuate the illusion of a flawless community, and deflect responsibility for shortcomings.

9. **Protecting a leader's ego:** Recognizing deviations may indicate that the leader's actions or leadership style contributed to dissatisfaction. By ignoring those who leave, the leader protects their ego from the recognition of fallibility and maintains a self-image of infallibility.

10. **Maintaining a sense of superiority:** Ignoring defections reinforces the narrative that those who leave are inferior or misled. The leader cultivates an environment where departure is seen as a personal failure, preserving the leader's sense of

superiority and the sect's supposed exclusivity.

Reconstructing Self-Esteem:

How Community Members Should Rebuild Their Own Self-Image After the Sect's Abandonment.

The Process of Healing:

The Steps to Recovery and Recovery after the Influence of a Narcissist.

The manipulation of spirituality by a narcissist in religious leadership is a critical aspect that can have a profound impact on a community's religious faith.

Manifestations of Spirituality:

Narcissistic leaders tend to use spirituality as a tool for their own agenda, and this manipulation manifests itself in multiple ways within a community.

1. Selected Revelations and Visions:

The leader may claim to have received exclusive revelations and visions from God, giving him a unique authority and leading role. This exclusivity can be used to cultivate a climate of dependency and to discourage any doubt or opposition.

2. Distortion of Spiritual Doctrines:

Narcissistic leaders may deliberately distort religious teachings to adapt them to their interests. This distortion can lead to a distortion of the community's understanding of spirituality and a departure from the true essence of their faith.

3. Control over Rituals and Practices:

The leader may exercise control over rituals and spiritual practices within the community. This control creates a climate where individuals depend on the leader for their spiritual experiences and expressions.

4. Misuse of Gift and Talents:

Narcissistic leaders can abuse the gifts and talents of community members for their own gain. For example, they may encourage individuals to give up their time, money, or skills under the pretext of religious sacrifice while the leader himself benefits.

5. Exclusivity of Divine Messages:

The leader may claim to be the only conduit for divine messages and that other voices or interpretations are unreliable. This exclusivity gives the leader a monopoly over the performance of divine guidance.

The Psychological Consequences of the Manipulation of Spirituality:

The manipulation of spirituality by a narcissist in religious leadership has a severe impact on the psychological well-being of community members.

1. Loss of Self-Determination:

Individuals may find themselves in a state of loss of self-determination, where they sacrifice their own spiritual journey and judgment for the leader's authority. This dependence can lead to a loss of individual identity.

2. Confusion about Spirituality:

The manipulation of spirituality can lead to confusion about the true nature of spirituality. Individuals may begin to doubt their spiritual experiences' sincerity and ability to develop a healthy and genuine faith life.

3. Emotional Dependence:

Community members may develop an unhealthy emotional dependence on the leader. This dependence can lead to a constant search for approval and confirmation of the leader, even at the expense of individual well-being.

4. Anxiety for Absence of Spirituality:

The leader can promote the idea that no true spirituality exists without him. This institution creates a climate where individuals fear following their spiritual path or developing their faith concept independently.

5. Social seclusion:

Individuals who begin to recognize the manipulation of spirituality may find themselves becoming socially isolated. This isolation is often a strategy to discourage any potential challenge to the leader's authority.

Structural Dynamics that Maintain the Manipulation of Spirituality:

The persistence of the manipulation of spirituality within a community is often underpinned by specific structural dynamics.

1. Hierarchical Structure:

A hierarchical structure in which the leader has unlimited authority contributes to the persistence of the manipulation of spirituality. Community members may find that they have little or no say in the spiritual direction of the community.

2. Limited Access to Information:

Limited access to objective information and alternative views reinforces the manipulation of spirituality. Individuals may find that they are limited to the data presented by the leader.

3. Lack of Accountability:

A lack of an effective accountability system makes it difficult for individuals to combat the leader's manipulation of spirituality. This lack of transparency makes it easier for the leader to continue his agenda without any challenge.

4. Peer Pressure and Affirmation:

Peer pressure and the quest for affirmation within the community can reinforce the manipulation of spirituality. Individuals may find themselves suppressing their own views to suit the prevailing groupthink.

5. Manipulation of Religious Doctrines:

The leader's manipulation of religious teachings to conform to his own agenda contributes to the persistence of the manipulation of spirituality. The leader may emphasize or distort certain doctrines to justify his own position.

Concluding Thoughts:

The manipulation of spirituality by a narcissist in religious leadership is a disruptive practice that can have a far-reaching impact on a community's spiritual well-being. This undermines the sincerity of religious belief and creates a climate of dependency and uncertainty. The awareness of these manifestations, their consequences, and the structural dynamics that maintain them are essential to promoting a healthy and authentic spiritual environment within a community.

Chapter 10: The Outcome and Future

Warning Signs: How to recognize a narcissistic leader before damage is done.

The Road to Recovery: Guidelines and support for those recovering from the influence of a narcissist.

Introduction:

The dynamics of community pressure is a critical aspect that supports the persistence of a narcissist in religious leadership.

This chapter examines how community pressure strengthens the leader's authority, including its manifestations, the psychological consequences for individuals, and the structural dynamics that sustain it.

Manifestations of Community Pressure:

Community pressure in the context of a narcissist in religious leadership takes several forms, revealing itself through specific manifestations.

1. Affirmation of the Leader's Authority:

The community may continuously facilitate affirmation of the leader's authority by accepting him as an unquestionable authority figure. This affirmation can be achieved through repeated public recognition, rituals of loyalty, and the undermining of any criticism.

2. Repulsion of Dissidents:

Dissidents within the community, individuals who openly stand up to or criticize the leader, may be exposed to ostracization. This social isolation serves as a warning to other community members to avoid opposition.

3. Groupthink and Conformism:

Promoting groupthink and conformism within the community encourages individuals to suppress their views and judgments and accept the prevailing group belief. This dynamic strengthens the leader's authority by promoting a uniform voice within the community.

4. Social Control and Judgment:

Maintaining social controls and a climate of judgment within the community contributes to suppressing alternative views and dissident voices. Community members may fear deviating from accepted norms and values.

5. Reward of Conformity:

Conformity to the leader's guidelines can be rewarded by favorable treatment, recognition, or access to unique benefits within the community. This reward reinforces the positive feedback run for those who adapt to the prevailing norms.

The Psychological Consequences of Community Pressure:

The pressure within the community to conform to the leader's authority clearly impacts the psychological well-being of individuals.

1. Anxiety of Isolation:

The fear of seclusion and loss of community bondage may force individuals to suppress their views and adapt to the prevailing groupthink. This fear can lead to constant anxiety about preserving social relationships.

2. Self-Censorship and Oppression:

Community members may begin to apply self-censorship and suppress their judgment to avoid criticism and seclusion. This self-limitation can lead to a suppression of individual expression and freedom of thought.

3. Identity Loss:

The constant pressure to adapt to the community's norms and the suppression of individual views can lead to a loss of personal identity. Individuals may sacrifice their values and beliefs to maintain a sense of community acceptance.

4. Emotional Dependence:

The dependence on the community's affirmation and approval can lead to an unhealthy emotional obsession. Community members may begin to believe that their value depends on the degree of acceptance within the community.

5. Suppression of Critical Thinking:

The pressure to conform can suppress critical thinking and the fear of questioning the leader's authority. This oppression hinders the healthy exchange of ideas within the community.

Structural Dynamics that Sustain Community Pressures:

The persistence of community pressure within a religious community is often underpinned by specific structural dynamics.

1. Hierarchical Structure:

A hierarchical structure in which the leader has excessive power contributes to the persistence of community pressure. Community members may feel that they have little influence on decision-making and policy within the community.

2. Control over Information and Communication:

The leader's control over information and communication is critical in maintaining community pressure. Limited access to alternative views and information can limit the community to the leader's narrative.

3. Peer Pressure and Affirmation:

Peer pressure and searching for confirmation can deter community members from considering alternative views. The fear of seclusion can be a powerful motivation to adapt to the prevailing groupthink.

4. Lack of Transparency and Accountability:

A lack of transparency and a flawed accountability system makes it difficult for individuals to stand up against community pressure. The leader may advance his agenda without any opposition.

5. Manipulation of Group Identity:

The leader may deliberately manipulate the group identity to create a strong sense of unity. This manipulation reinforces community pressure by making individuals believe they are part of an exclusive and necessary community.

Concluding Thoughts:

Community pressure in the context of a narcissist in religious leadership is a powerful tool that supports the persistence of the leader's authority. This creates a climate of conformism, oppression, and fear of seclusion. Awareness of these manifestations, their effects, and the structural dynamics that maintain them are essential to fostering a healthy and inclusive community.

Chapter 11 - A sect/church leader with a narcissistic personality can use finances in various ways to manipulate and oppress individuals.

1. **Financial Dependency:** The leader can create an environment where individuals depend financially on the cult/church and its leader. It can be created by a system in which members transfer their finances or assets to the cult/church or convince them to make sufficient contributions to achieve a specific status or "spiritual benefit" within the group.

A sect/church leader with a narcissistic personality can use finances in various ways to manipulate and oppress individuals.

Here are some of the strategic approaches often seen:

- **Accumulating Wealth for the Leader:** A narcissistic leader may pursue an extravagant lifestyle and use the financial means of the cult/church for personal gain. This can be luxury properties, exclusive vehicles, or other status symbols. Members can be encouraged to make contributions through the promise of spiritual rewards.
- **Manipulation of Offerings:** The leader may use offerings or contributions as a measure of devotion. Members may become convinced that a higher financial contribution to the cult/church will increase spiritual well-being or even a special status within the group.
- **Financial Punitive Measures:** Individuals who do not make adequate contributions may be exposed to financial punitive measures. This could include excluding them from specific benefits or opportunities or even public humiliation due to

their perceived lack of commitment.

- **The illusion of Financial Prosperity:** The leader can create an illusion of financial prosperity within the cult/church, where members become convinced that their financial contributions lead to a common goal and benefit the entire community. This perception can be used to motivate individuals to make more contributions.

- **Use of Guilt and Guilt:** A narcissistic leader can manipulate guilt by convincing members that they have a moral or spiritual obligation to make significant financial sacrifices for the cult/church's greater purpose. The leader uses possible feelings of guilt to maintain checks and promote further contributions.

By manipulating financial means, a narcissistic leader can create an environment in which individuals are not only financially dependent but also psychologically oppressed and motivated to contribute continuously. This dynamic maintains the leader's authority and the cult/church's control over its members.

1. **Accumulating Wealth for the Leader:** A narcissistic leader may pursue an extravagant lifestyle and use the financial means of the cult for personal gain. This can be luxury properties, exclusive vehicles, or other status symbols. Members can be encouraged to make contributions through the promise of spiritual rewards.

- **Spiritual Benefits:** The leader of the sect, with a narcissistic tendency, can promise extraordinary spiritual benefits to those who make sufficient financial sacrifices. These promises can vary from a heightened spiritual awareness to attaining a higher form of salvation or enlightenment.

These benefits may be linked to specific financial contributions, and individuals become convinced that giving more will give them a higher level of spiritual enlightenment.

- **Elevated Status:** Members may be reminded that a higher level of financial contribution leads to spiritual rewards and an increased status within the community. This can be regarded as a sign of higher devotion and dignity in fellow members' eyes.

- **Individual Predictions:** The leader can make individual predictions about the spiritual benefits a member may experience due to specific financial contributions. These personalized promises create a sense of personal goals and desire to obtain these benefits.

- **Anxiety of Exclusion:** Members may fear that a lack of financial contribution or a reduction thereof could lead to exclusion from specific spiritual opportunities or rituals, negatively impacting their spiritual well-being.

- **Use of Emotions:** These promises are often linked to manipulating emotions, including the fear of being shut out, the desire for spiritual fulfillment, and the hope of a better life. This emotional manipulation indicates that financial contributions can only achieve the desired spiritual benefits.

1. **Manipulation of Offerings:** The leader may use offerings or contributions as a measure of devotion. Members may become convinced that a higher financial contribution to the cult/church will increase spiritual well-being or even a special status within the group.

- **Connection between Finance and Spiritual Well-Being:** A narcissistic sect/church leader can create a direct link between a member's financial contributions and his or her spiritual well-being. Members may become convinced that higher contributions lead to a more blessed or fulfilled spiritual life. In contrast, a lack of financial commitment may lead to a deterioration in spiritual well-being.

- **Anxiety of Spiritual Slippage:** Individuals may have feared that a lack of financial contributions would land them in a state of spiritual slippage. This fear can be fed by the leader's predictions or threats about the spiritual dangers of a decline in financial commitment.

- **Manipulation by Uncertainty:** Sect/church leaders with a narcissistic slant can consciously use uncertainty to manipulate members. For example, they might say that the spiritual path is suspenseful. Still, individuals can ensure security and well-being in the afterlife by making adequate financial contributions.

- **Disapproval of Financial Withdrawal:** If a member is considering withdrawing financially, the leader may see this action as a lack of commitment to the spiritual calling. Members may then fear that a decrease in financial contributions will lead directly to disapproval of the leader and a reduction in their spiritual status.

- **Use of Guilt:** The leader can manipulate guilt by convincing members that the cult/church's spiritual mission depends on each individual's contributions. If they do not contribute enough, they may be persuaded that they bear personal responsibility for any failure or ordeal within the cult/church.

- **Vulnerability of Personal Spirituality:** The leader can emphasize the exposure of an individual's personal spirituality and then say that this vulnerability can be protected and strengthened through sufficient financial contributions. This strategy can appeal to people's longing to find spiritual security.

The threat of a decline in spiritual well-being is a powerful tool in the hands of a narcissistic leader to enforce financial obedience. This manipulation takes advantage of emotional security and fear of spiritual loss, which enables the leader to maintain a control-oriented culture and encourages members to continually make financial contributions.

1. **Financial Punitive Measures:** Individuals who do not make adequate contributions may be exposed to financial punitive measures. This could include excluding them from specific benefits or opportunities or even public humiliation due to their perceived lack of commitment.

- **Exclusion of Benefits:** Sect/church leaders with a narcissistic tendency may consider the use of financial punitive measures to maintain discipline within the community. For example, individuals who do not make adequate financial contributions may be excluded from specific rituals, events, or even an accessible circle within the cult that is considered privileged status.
- **Public humiliation:** If members do not make the expected financial contributions, the leader may consider publicly humiliating them. This humiliation can occur within the community, during rituals, or even in public. This attempts to intimidate and discourage other members from doing the same.
- **Isolation and Exclusion:** If an individual persists with decreased financial contributions, the leader may consider applying isolation or exclusion. These measures serve not only as a punishment but also as an example to other members of what can happen if they do not meet financial expectations.
- **Loss of Favors:** The leader may use a member's fear of losing favors or approval to motivate them to meet financial

obligations. These obligations are a measure of loyalty and devotion to the cult.

- **The threat of Spiritual Punishment:** A narcissistic leader may also be threatened with spiritual punitive measures, such as the ability to achieve spiritual growth or the possibility of a negative afterlife experience if individuals do not contribute adequately.

- **Permanent Stamp of Distinction:** Individuals may bear a permanent stamp of distinction if they do not meet financial expectations. This stamp can signify a lack of commitment within the cult/church's community.

Using punitive financial measures is often an effective way to control members by cultivating a sphere of fear and submission. The threat of negative consequences linked to economic disobedience is a powerful tool the leader can use to ensure loyalty and obedience within the community.

1. **The illusion of Financial Prosperity:** The leader can create an illusion of financial prosperity within the cult, where members become convinced that their financial contributions lead to a common goal and benefit the entire community. This perception can be used to motivate individuals to make more contributions.

- **View of the Leader as Divine:** A narcissistic leader may regard himself or herself as a divine figure or guided by a divine power. This view of the leader's sacred position is often linked to the idea that his or her financial guidelines are determined by a higher power.

- **Believe in a Divine Plan:** Members become convinced that the cult/church's financial system is part of a divine plan. The leader may claim that God inspired him or her to establish a specific economic structure and that members participate in this plan through their contributions.

- **Financial Contributions as a Divine Duty:** The leader may view financial contributions as a divine duty required of the members to fulfill their spiritual calling. Members are persuaded that their economic sacrifices are a part of their spiritual service to God.

- **Use of Religious Terminology:** The leader may use religious terminology to envelop the financial system of the cult. For example, "sacrifice" may be used instead of "contribution," and the leader may claim that these sacrifices are a sacred act that serves a spiritual purpose.

- **Linking Divine Approval to Financial Contributions:** The leader may imply that divine approval and blessing are directly tied to the scope of an individual's financial contributions. This linkage reinforces the idea that economic obedience is a spiritual necessity.

- **Threatening with Divine Punishment:** There may be a threat of divine punishment for those who do not make adequate financial contributions. Members may have feared that disobeying the leader's financial guidelines could lead to divine wrath.

This strategy uses members' religious beliefs to justify and motivate financial contributions. The leader uses faith in a divine direction to sanctify the financial system and to create a climate of religious obedience, leading to loyalty and assistance within the community.

1. **Use of Guilt and Guilt:** A narcissistic leader can manipulate guilt by convincing members that they have a moral or spiritual obligation to make significant financial sacrifices for the cult's greater purpose. The leader uses possible feelings of guilt to maintain checks and promote further contributions.

- **Guilt as a Control Tool:** A narcissistic leader can deliberately use guilt as a control tool to guide the behavior of individuals within the cult. Members may be insinuated into believing that any form of deviation from financial norms is a grave sin and should lead to feelings of guilt.
- **Self-Inquiry and Control:** Members may be encouraged to constantly self-examine their financial contributions and to judge themselves against the measure of the cult/church's norms. This self-examination and control is a part of the leader's strategy to create an internal voice of criticism and promote a self-regulatory dynamic.
- **Individual Responsibility for Financial Affairs:** Members may be taught to take personal responsibility for their financial affairs within the cult. Any economic challenges or uncertainties can be attributed to the individual rather than structural problems within the cult/church.
- **Guilt as a Dissociation Tool:** Guilt can also be a dissociating agent within the community. Individuals may have feared speaking openly about their doubts or views for fear of guilt or condemnation from other members.
- **Debt as a Motivator:** Members may be taught that the only way to get rid of feelings of guilt is by faithfully making financial contributions. The promise of an enlightened mind and a clear conscience may motivate members to meet financial obligations.
- **Public Confession of Guilt:** Members may be encouraged to openly confess any guilt related to financial matters. These public confessions can serve as a form of self-correcting discipline and can also serve as a warning to others.

Guilt is a psychological tactic that helps the leader maintain a controlled and obedient community. Individuals may fear deviating from financial norms, which can have economic consequences, social disapproval, and guilt within the community. This dynamic maintains the leader's control over the financial aspects of the cult.

By manipulating financial means, a narcissistic leader can create an environment in which individuals are not only financially dependent but also psychologically oppressed and motivated to contribute continuously. This dynamic maintains the leader's authority and the cult's control over its members.

Chapter 12 - Retaining Financial Control:

The leader can maintain sustainable financial control by keeping the financial statements secret. One can decide what information is shared, with whom, and when to support a suitable narrative.

A narcissistic sect/church leader may have a solid motivation to prevent financial statements from being made public, and here are a few reasons why:

Control and Power:

By keeping the financial statements secret, the leader retains high control and power within the cult/church. This allows him or her to manage the financial means of the cult for his own sake without any external testing.

Avoid criticism and scrutiny:

The disclosure of financial statements can lead to external criticism, scrutiny by government institutions, and even possible legal issues. A narcissistic leader often does not want to have his or her actions or financial management questioned and may attempt to avoid outside criticism.

Preservation of Image:

Sect/church leaders with narcissistic personalities often care about their public image and performance. Disclosure of financial statements may create potential negative perceptions, and the leader's authority or divine status in the eyes of his or her followers may be threatened.

Conceal financial wrongs:

If there is any form of financial wrongdoing or misuse of funds within the cult/church, disclosing it would have severe consequences for the leader. The leader may prefer to keep the financial statements secret to avoid this risk.

Preventing Unlocking Financial Strategies:

The leader may employ particular financial strategies or practices that would not be favorable if made public. By keeping the financial statements secret, the leader prevents these strategies from coming to light.

Avoid Unlocking Personal Financial Status:

Narcissistic leaders may pursue a luxurious lifestyle, and disclosing personal financial information, such as high incomes or wealth, can raise questions about the integrity of the leader's spiritual message or sacrifices.

These reasons point to the narcissistic leader's desire to maintain control, avoid external criticism, and protect his or her own interests and image by keeping the sect's financial statements secret. This contributes to building a culture of secrecy and obedience within the community.

Chapter 13 Empowering Individuals to Leave a Narcissist-Led Sect/Church: A Comprehensive Approach

Introduction:

Leaving a sect headed by a narcissist is a complex and delicate process that requires a multifaceted approach. A comprehensive plan can be implemented to empower individuals to make informed decisions about leaving such sects by addressing psychological, emotional, legal, and community aspects.

1. **Education and awareness campaigns:**

The development of educational materials and awareness campaigns is a fundamental step. These resources should outline the characteristics of narcissistic leaders, manipulation tactics used in such sects/churches, and the potential consequences for members. Different media, such as pamphlets, online content, and workshops, can reach a broad audience.

Education should focus on cultivating critical thinking skills and encourage individuals to question the authority and practices within the sect/church. Providing clear information about the traits of narcissistic leaders helps individuals recognize manipulative behaviors, fostering an environment where members feel empowered to question their involvement.

2. **Hotlines and support networks:**

Establishing hotlines and support networks is crucial to providing immediate assistance to those considering leaving a sect/church. Trained counselors, ideally individuals with experience in cult recovery or mental health professionals, can offer a confidential space for individuals to share their concerns, ask questions, and receive emotional support.

These hotlines can serve as a lifeline for individuals who feel isolated or trapped, providing a non-judgmental space to express their doubts and fears. The support networks can extend to online forums, allowing members to connect with others who have successfully left similar situations, fostering a sense of community and understanding.

3. Safe spaces for dialogue:

Creating safe spaces for open dialogue is essential for breaking down the barriers of fear and isolation that often accompany sect engagement. Both online forums and in-person support groups can provide platforms for individuals to share their experiences without judgment.

These spaces should be moderated by professionals trained in cult recovery or mental health to ensure a supportive and constructive environment. Open dialogue allows individuals to examine their doubts, gain insights from others, and gradually build up the courage to consider leaving the sect.

4. Counseling and Therapy Services:

Offering counseling and therapy services tailored to the experiences of sect members is a critical component of the plan. Mental health professionals who specialize in cult restoration can provide targeted support, helping individuals come to terms with the emotional and psychological toll of such a sect.

Therapy sessions can address the manipulation tactics used by narcissistic leaders, examine the impact on an individual's sense of self, and develop coping strategies for the challenges of leaving. These services must be accessible and affordable to ensure widespread availability.

5. Legal Aid:

Cooperation with lawyers is essential to inform individuals of their rights and legal options when leaving a sect. Workshops and briefings can educate sect members about the legal protections available and dispel any misinformation or fear associated with legal consequences.

Lawyers can provide pro bono services or discounted rates to sect members seeking assistance, ensuring that costs are not a barrier to accessing legal advice. Empowering individuals with knowledge about their legal rights can instill confidence and reduce the anxiety associated with leaving.

6. Family and Community Outreach:

Getting involved with the families and communities of sect members is a proactive approach to creating a supportive environment for those considering leaving. Workshops and educational programs can be organized to help families understand the dynamics of sects led by narcissists and the challenges faced by their loved ones.

Building understanding and empathy within these circles is essential for establishing a safety net for individuals who choose to leave. Family members can provide emotional support and encouragement during the transition.

7. **Rehabilitation Programs:**

The development of rehabilitation programs is a forward-looking initiative to help individuals reintegrate into mainstream society after leaving a sect. These programs should address individuals' psychological, social, and practical challenges during this transition.

Rehabilitation programs may include therapy sessions, vocational training, and community support to help individuals rebuild their lives. Collaborating with existing rehabilitation services and mental health professionals ensures a comprehensive and well-rounded approach.

8. **Media Exposure:**

Media awareness is a powerful tool to shine a light on the practices of narcissistic leaders and their impact on sect members. Documentaries, news features, and interviews with former members can provide valuable insights into the inner workings of such sects.

Media exposure serves a dual purpose: it teaches the public about the dangers of narcissistic sects. It can serve as a catalyst for individuals within the sect to question their involvement. Media coverage also creates a platform for individuals to share their stories, contributing to a broader societal dialogue.

9. **Exit counseling:**

Providing specialized exit counseling services is a hands-on approach to helping individuals navigate the complexities of leaving a sect. Exit counseling sessions, conducted by professionals experienced in cult restoration, aim to help individuals clear their minds, address cognitive dissonance, and make informed decisions about their future.

These sessions may involve cognitive behavioral techniques, counseling on family dynamics, and practical advice on rebuilding one's life outside the sect. Exit counseling should be offered with empathy and respect for the individual's autonomy.

10. **Community Education Workshops:**

Conducting community workshops is an essential step in preventing the recruitment of new members and fostering an environment of awareness and support. These workshops should educate communities about narcissistic leaders' manipulation tactics and equip followers to recognize warning signs.

Community education empowers individuals to identify and intervene when someone they know is at risk of falling victim to a narcissistic-led sect. Creating an informed and vigilant community increases the chances of intervention before someone becomes deeply involved.

Conclusion:

A comprehensive plan to help individuals leave a narcissistic-led sect involves a strategic combination of education, emotional support, legal assistance, and community involvement. Recognizing individuals' psychological and emotional challenges is crucial to tailoring effective interventions that respect their autonomy. This multifaceted approach aims to facilitate the exit from such sects and empower individuals to rebuild their lives and reintegrate them into society.

Chapter 14: Counseling for Individuals under a Narcissistic Leader

Introduction:

Serving in the shadow of a narcissistic leader can be a challenging and emotionally taxing experience. This chapter aims to offer practical advice for individuals who are disregarded and hurt by a narcissistic leader. The counseling models at the end of the chapter serve as a supplement, where multiple approaches are discussed to support individuals in their journey to recovery.

The Psychological Challenges of Serving under a Narcissistic Leader:

1. Recognition of the Situation:

One of the most significant psychological challenges that individuals face in a narcissistic environment is the difficulty of **acknowledging the true nature** of the situation. This recognition is often linked to emotional resistance and can have deeply ingrained consequences for an individual's self-identity.

In a narcissistic environment, the individual is often confronted with the leader's subtle manipulation of reality. Gaslighting, a tactic where the leader tries to control the individual's perception through the spread of confusion and doubt, plays a cardinal role in this phase. This manipulation makes it difficult for the individual to see the dysfunctionality of the environment.

The process of recognition requires an inner struggle between what the individual is experiencing and the false reality created by the narcissist. This dissonance can take a considerable emotional toll, with feelings of insecurity, self-doubt, and even guilt playing a prominent role. Awareness and self-reflection are essential to overcome this challenge. This may involve actively researching narcissism and manipulation tactics and even enlisting professional help to deepen awareness.

2. Handling Gaslight Tactics:

Gaslighting by a narcissistic leader is a subtle but powerful psychological tool. It involves the manipulation of the perception of the individual, which leads to confusion, uncertainty, and a distortion of reality. Dealing with these tactics requires an analysis of the dynamics between the leader and the individual's psyche.

One of the most prominent gaslighting techniques is projection, where the narcissist attributes his own negative properties to the individual. This projection creates an environment in which the individual must constantly self-examine and doubt one's intuition. If an individual can clearly identify this tactic, it can lessen its impact.

A further gaslighting technique is blaming, where the narcissist places responsibility for adverse events on the individual. This sabotage of an individual's self-esteem can lead to guilt and self-criticism. The individual must decode these dynamics and cultivate self-forgiveness.

Dealing with gaslight tactics also requires establishing healthy boundaries. The narcissist's lack of respect for personal space and rights can trample the individual's boundaries, which can lead to a sense of loss of self-control. By consciously and deliberately setting boundaries, the individual can begin to reduce the impact of the gaslight.

3. Self-preservation and setting boundaries:

Dealing with a narcissistic leader's environment calls for an active process of self-preservation and establishing healthy boundaries. This psychological challenge has its roots in the power struggle between the narcissist's craving for control and the individual's need for self-protection.

Self-preservation within a narcissistic environment means maintaining the awareness of one's own emotional state and needs. This awareness may arise by actively identifying emotions and determining when boundaries are transcended. This is a process of emotional intelligence, where the individual learns to recognize emotions and deal with them effectively.

Setting boundaries in a narcissistic environment is a strategic psychological step. It involves the precise and deliberate communication of personal boundaries and the individual's point of view within the environment. These boundaries can include emotional boundaries, such as refusing to participate in negative interactions, and physical boundaries to preserve personal space.

Another aspect of this psychological challenge is the association with the narcissist's response to the establishment of boundaries. Narcissists often cannot accept boundaries, and they may try to transcend those boundaries through manipulative behavior. This phase of self-preservation and boundaries calls for strengthening inner self-confidence and self-respect.

4. Distinguish between Self-Worth and Narcissistic Evaluations:

A critical psychological challenge within a narcissistic environment is the tendency of the individual to link self-worth to the judgment of the narcissist. Narcissists, with their excess selfishness and need for admiration, create an environment in which individuals are constantly judged and criticized.

The individual may begin to accept the narcissist's views of themselves as the measure of self-worth. This internalization of the narcissistic narrative can shape an increase in self-doubt, self-criticism, and self-song.

To overcome this psychological challenge, it is essential to make a clear distinction between one's own worth and the narcissistic evaluations.

The process of discernment calls for inner work on self-appreciation and self-love. This may include consciously adopting positive self-talk and actively refuting negative self-criticism.

Self-care practices, such as meditation on the Word of God and affirmations, can help promote a positive self-image and reduce the influence of narcissistic criticism.

Another aspect of this psychological challenge is the recognition of the manipulative nature of the narcissist's evaluations. Narcissists often use criticism as a tactic to exert control and subjugate others. By identifying these manipulation tactics, the individual can begin to look at the criticism objectively and not accept it as a valuable measure of themselves.

Practical Steps for Handling:
Strive for External Support:

- Seek support outside the narcissistic environment. Contact friends, family, or professional counselors to establish a supportive network. External perspectives can help confirm the reality of the situation and provide a source of emotional support.

Clear communication:

- Try to maintain clear, concise communication when interacting with the narcissist. Avoid unnecessary conflict and try to limit emotional engagement. Communicate only essential information and keep the interaction as objective as possible.

Self-Care and Emotional Recovery:

- Focus on self-care and emotional recovery. Meditation on God's Word, exercise, and art therapy can help reduce stress and promote self-awareness. Do not lose sight of the importance of your own well-being.

Develop a Strong Exterior:

- To resist the emotional manipulation of a narcissistic leader, it is crucial to develop a strong exterior. These include self-assurance and a determined attitude to the toxic dynamics.

Chapter 15: Counseling Models for Recovery:

This Chapter examines four counseling models that individuals who have been disregarded and hurt by a narcissistic leader can use for recovery. These models have multiple approaches and focus areas, each designed to address the unique psychological challenges of this situation.

Model 1: Cognitive Behaviour Counselling (KGC):

KGC is an approach that focuses on identifying and changing negative thoughts and behavior patterns. Within the context of a narcissistic environment, this model can be a precious tool for addressing negative self-esteem and self-sabotaging behavior.

Cognitive Aspect:

This aspect of KGC involves raising awareness and identifying negative self-talk and self-sabotaging thinking. Because of the narcissistic environment, individuals may develop an internal dialogue that undermines their self-worth. KGC helps identify these thoughts and replace them with positive, affirmative self-talk.

Behavioral Aspect:

The behavioral aspect of KGC focuses on changing self-sabotaging behavior. This may include behaviors encouraged by the narcissist, such as self-sacrificing behavior or an inability to set boundaries. KGC provides tools and strategies to recognize and change these patterns of behavior.

Exposure to Positive Experiences:

Another element of KGC is the gradual exposure to positive experiences to establish new, healthier behavioral patterns. These can be inclusive in building self-confidence through successful achievements, developing healthy social relationships, and adopting self-care practices.

Model 2: Emotional Intelligence Counseling (EIC):

EIC is an approach focused on developing emotional awareness and emotional intelligence. For individuals who have been manipulated by a narcissistic leader, EIC can help strengthen their emotional coping and promote awareness of other people's emotions.

Awareness of Emotions:

The key to EIC is the awareness of the full spectrum of emotions. For individuals who have gone through a narcissistic environment, there may be suppression of emotions due to gaslight tactics. EIC encourages an active recognition of these emotions.

Coping with Emotions:

This aspect of EIC focuses on developing skills to deal effectively with emotions. This includes identifying healthy ways to deal with negative emotions, including relaxation techniques, meditation, and other self-care practices.

Empathic communication:

A critical element of EIC is the promotion of empathic communication. This skill is essential for individuals who may be inclined to suppress their own emotions while being sensitive to the feelings of others. EIC helps strike a balance between empathy and self-protection.

Model 3: Narrative Therapy:

Narrative therapy is an approach that encourages individuals to retell their own stories and develop a new perspective. For those manipulated by a narcissistic leader, this model can initiate a recovery process through the creation of a new frame of meaning.

Retelling Story:

Narrative therapy encourages individuals to retell events within the narcissistic setting. This retelling is an opportunity to give the experiences a new meaning and develop a more nuanced view of the self.

Identifying Strength:

A key focus of this model is identifying individual strengths and resilience. For individuals who may have been undermined by the narcissistic environment, recognizing their strengths is a critical element in the recovery process.

Creative Self-Expression:

Narrative therapy encourages creative self-expression, including writing, drawing, or other forms of art therapy. These innovative processes help individuals express their emotions and provide an alternative way to process those experiences.

Model 4: Systemic Counseling:

Systemic counseling examines the social context in which individuals operate. For those manipulated by a narcissistic leader, systemic counseling can help repair interpersonal relationships and build a supportive community.

Dealing with Interpersonal Relationships:

The critical component of systemic counseling is interpersonal relationships within the individual's social sphere. These can be inclusive when repairing torn family ties, building new friendships, and establishing supportive communities.

Family dynamics:

For individuals manipulated by a narcissistic leader, systemic counseling can explore family dynamics and help restore healthy communication patterns. It focuses on identifying dysfunctional dynamics and promoting healthy interactions.

Social Support:

An essential aspect of systemic counseling is the encouragement of social support. This includes identifying trusted social networks that can support the individual through recovery. This may consist of participating in support groups or community activities.

Concluding Thoughts:

These counseling models provide a diversity of approaches to support individuals who have been disregarded and hurt by narcissistic leaders. While each model addresses unique aspects of the recovery process, it is crucial to take a holistic approach that considers the special needs and contexts of the individual. This may involve integrating various models depending on the specific circumstances and the progress of the recovery process.

Counseling models can play a valuable role in supporting individuals who serve under a narcissistic leader and exposing them to emotional abuse. It is essential to take an approach that addresses each individual's unique needs and leverage a range of resources to promote a comprehensive recovery. By taking practical steps and mastering the necessary self-care, individuals can begin to free themselves from the negative impact of their experience within a narcissistic environment.

Chapter 16: Various ways a narcissistic leader uses to not take responsibility

Manipulation through Intimidation

Threat and intimidation is one of the critical aspects of DARVO that a narcissistic leader uses to evade responsibility. This strategy involves the use of intimidation, warnings, and sometimes even outright threats to put the person accusing him in a position of fear and uncertainty.

A narcissistic leader's threats can range from subtle to overtly aggressive. Subtle threats can be inclusive when suggesting potential adverse effects on the person, such as the implication of personal or professional harm. It can concern their career, reputation, or personal relationships.

More overt threats may include direct consistencies, such as dismissal, discrediting, or other reprisals. This tactic increases a person's fear of negative consequences, holding them back from further revelations or accusations.

An example of a threat in this context is a narcissistic leader who threatens an individual who accuses him of misconduct with the disclosure of personal information that could damage the person's reputation or career.

Deny: Manipulation by Negation

Denial is a critical stage in the DARVO strategy used by a narcissistic leader. This phase involves the direct or indirect denial of his involvement in the alleged misconduct. This tactic was designed to preserve his self-esteem and reputation by refuting the allegations.

A narcissistic leader can use this tactic through a variation of denial strategies:

1. **Direct Denial:**
    ◦ The leader can simply reject the allegations, claiming

they have no truth. He can say that the allegations are false or in any way misleading. It serves as an attempt to deny and suppress the negative perception of itself.

2. **Minimization:**
   ◦ A narcissistic leader may try to minimize the seriousness of the allegations. This may include claiming that the specified misconduct is not essential or is not serious. This strategy is designed to reduce the impact of the allegations.

3. **Blame shifted:**
   ◦ A further denial strategy is to shift the blame to others. The narcissistic leader may say that other individuals, circumstances, or factors cause the situation. This helps him evade his own responsibility and put the focus elsewhere.

An example of denial is when a narcissistic leader directly denies the allegations and dismisses the accusation as sheer defamation. He may also try to ignore the situation as minor and unimportant.

Role Reversal: Manipulation through Victimhood

Role reversal is the final stage of the DARVO strategy that narcissistic leaders use to evade responsibility. This phase involves reversing the roles, where the narcissistic leader tries to present himself as the genuine victim. This tactic is designed to garner sympathy, sow doubts, and distract attention from his own misconduct.

A narcissistic leader can use this tactic by:

1. **Self-compassion:**
   - He may see himself as the one affected by unjust accusations. By cultivating an image of himself as an innocent victim, he tries to change the negative perception.

2. **Accusation of Others:**
   - The leader may try to accuse others of conspiring against him. This tactic is designed to distract attention from his own misconduct by creating the semblance of a plot.

3. **Emotional manipulation:**
   - He may also use emotional manipulation by demonstrating self-compassion, sadness, or even anger. These emotional reactions serve as an attempt to garner sympathy from others and to convince them of his innocence.

An example of role reversal is when a narcissistic leader claims to be the real victim in a situation where he is accused of misconduct. He can say that he is being unfairly attacked and that others have an agenda against him. This tactic is designed to protect itself and preserve its own image.

An example of how the DARVO phenomenon is used in everyday society:

Imagine there is a corporate environment where a narcissistic executive named Pete is accused of unethical practices, including manipulation of financial information for personal gain.

Here's how Pete can use the DARVO strategy:

1. **Threaten:**
   - After the accusation becomes public, Pete meets with the employee who accuses him, Jane. During the meeting, Pete threatened disciplinary action, including possible dismissal, if she did not retract the accusations. He warns her that her career is in serious jeopardy and that he will take the necessary steps to protect his reputation.

Deny: Denial of Unethical Practices

1. **Deny:**
   - During the meeting, Pete denied any unethical practices. He says there is no truth in the accusations and that Jane tries to harm him by telling lies. Pete minimizes the seriousness of the allegations by saying that this is simply an attempt to call his integrity into question.

Role reversal: Representation of Pete as the Victim

1. **Role reversal:**
   - Pete turns the situation around to garner sympathy and divert attention from his misbehavior. He accused Jane of a personal vendetta against him, claiming she was trying to harm his reputation. Pete presents himself as innocently attacked, while Jane is an unreliable source.

Other methods, excluding DARVO, are used by a narcissistic leader to escape responsibility:

Threatening: Manipulating through Intimidation

1. **Threaten:**
   - The narcissistic leader can use threats as a tactic to bring the person accusing him into a state of fear and uncertainty. This may include threats of professional harm, disciplinary actions, or even personal retaliation. These threats are meant to deter the individual from further revelations or accusations.

Deny: Manipulation by Negation

1. **Deny:**
   - Denial is a critical phase where the narcissistic leader directly or indirectly denies his involvement in the alleged misconduct. He can dismiss the accusations as false or misleading and claim no truth. This tactic aims to protect his reputation by fending off the allegations.

Role reversal: Manipulation through Victimhood

1. **Role reversal:**
    - ○ Role reversal is the final stage, where the narcissistic leader tries to present himself as the victim in the situation. Through self-compassion, accusation of a plot against him, or demonstrations of emotional manipulation, he tries to garner sympathy from others. This phase is intended to divert attention from his own misconduct by drawing attention to him as those who are unfairly attacked.

These methods, applied within the framework of the DARVO strategy, create a complex pattern of manipulation that the narcissistic leader uses to evade responsibility and protect his own interests.

1. Gaslighting: Distorting Reality for Manipulation

Gaslighting is a manipulative tactic employed by narcissistic leaders to distort reality and make others doubt their own perceptions, memories, or sanity. This insidious form of psychological manipulation can have profound effects on the accuser's mental well-being and ability to assert the truth.

In a workplace scenario, a narcissistic leader might subtly alter details of past events, question the accuser's memory, or flat-out deny occurrences. They could employ phrases like "I never said that" or "You're imagining things" to create confusion. Gaslighting aims to erode the victim's confidence and make them increasingly reliant on the manipulator for a sense of reality.

This tactic is about denying specific events and creating an atmosphere of uncertainty and self-doubt. By systematically undermining the accuser's perception of reality, the narcissistic leader seeks to maintain control and divert attention from their own culpability.

2. Diversion Tactics: Shifting Focus to Maintain Control

Diversion tactics involve redirecting attention away from the accusations, often by creating alternative focal points or crises within the organization. When faced with allegations, a narcissistic leader may intentionally amplify other issues, instigate conflicts, or highlight external challenges to shift the organizational focus.

For example, they might initiate a sudden restructuring, emphasize a seemingly urgent crisis, or exploit pre-existing tensions. By doing so, the leader creates a chaotic environment where dealing with immediate concerns takes precedence over investigating the accusations. This strategy not only buys time but also diffuses the intensity of scrutiny, making it more challenging for the accuser to maintain momentum.

3. Character Assassination: Undermining Credibility for Self-Preservation

Character assassination is a method where the narcissistic leader attempts to discredit the accuser by tarnishing their reputation. This can involve spreading rumors, questioning the accuser's credibility, or highlighting any perceived flaws in their character.

In the workplace, the leader may exploit any available weaknesses or past mistakes of the accuser. They could gossip, subtly undermining the accuser's professional achievements or personal integrity. By creating doubt about the accuser's motives or reliability, the narcissistic leader aims to shift the focus from their actions to discrediting the messenger.

This tactic not only serves to undermine the credibility of the accuser but also creates a climate where others may hesitate to support or believe the allegations against the narcissistic leader.

4. Playing the Victim Card: Seeking Sympathy for Manipulation

In addition to the role reversal aspect of DARVO, the narcissistic leader may more overtly **play the victim card**. They cast themselves as unjustly accused, unfairly targeted, or even bullied by the accuser. This tactic is a strategic move to elicit sympathy and support from others in the organization.

The leader might emphasize the personal toll the accusations are taking on them, framing themselves as emotionally wounded or betrayed. They could appeal to colleagues, superiors, or subordinates, portraying themselves as a target of a malicious campaign. By manipulating emotions and garnering empathy, the narcissistic leader aims to create an environment where others are hesitant to challenge or question them.

This victim-playing tactic serves as a shield, deflecting attention from the substance of the accusations to an emotional narrative where the leader is perceived as the underdog fighting against injustice.

5. Selective Memory: Creating Uncertainty Through Forgetfulness

Selective memory is a tactic where the narcissistic leader conveniently forgets or denies specific events related to the accusations. This calculated amnesia creates uncertainty, making it challenging for others to establish a clear timeline of events or hold the leader accountable for their actions.

The leader may claim ignorance about crucial details, events, or conversations central to the accusations. They might say things like, "I don't recall saying that," or "I don't remember that meeting happening." This intentional forgetfulness is designed to create a fog of ambiguity, making it difficult for others to determine the accuracy of the accusations.

By selectively remembering or forgetting details, the narcissistic leader aims to sow seeds of doubt and prevent a cohesive narrative from forming around the allegations.

6. Manipulative Charm: Winning Over Through Charisma

Manipulative charm is a tactic where the narcissistic leader uses their charisma and social skills to win people over and create a positive image. When facing accusations, they may intensify their charm offensive to create a favorable perception that counters the adverse claims.

The leader may engage in excessive flattery, demonstrate apparent empathy, or showcase a charismatic persona to distract from the allegations. They could leverage their interpersonal skills to build alliances and support within the organization. Doing so creates an environment where others find it challenging to reconcile the charismatic leader they know with the damaging accusations.

This charm offensive is not just about superficial charm but also involves strategic interpersonal manipulation to ensure others are less inclined to believe or support the accuser.

In summary, when utilized with or separately from DARVO, these manipulative tactics constitute a comprehensive strategy employed by narcissistic leaders to sidestep responsibility, protect their image, and maintain control within the organizational context.

Counseling models for the treatment of Narcissism:

1. Individual Therapy: Profound Personal Recognition and Growth

Individual therapy for a narcissistic leader provides an environment within which the leader can develop personal awareness and deep recognition of self.

Here's a more detailed look at how this approach can be applied:

Cognitive behavioral therapy (CBT) in individual therapy:

CRT focuses on the connection between thoughts, feelings, and behaviors. For a narcissistic leader, this approach can help identify the negative thought patterns that lead to problematic behaviors. During individual therapy, the narcissistic leader will work with a therapist to address the following aspects:

- **Awareness of Thoughts:**
    - Identifying self-sabotaging or dysfunctional thoughts and beliefs that can drive narcissistic behavior.
- **Changing Thought Patterns:**
    - Development of healthier thought patterns and beliefs that promote a more realistic and positive self-image.
- **Handling Emotions:**
    - Learning skills for effectively managing emotions without resorting to narcissistic defenses.

Emotional intelligence therapy in individual therapy:

Emotional Intelligence (EI) plays a critical role in developing emotional awareness and effectively managing emotions. For a narcissistic leader, EI therapy may include:

- **Identifying Emotions:**
    - Learn to identify the range of emotions, including those often repressed.
- **Expression of Emotions:**
    - Development of healthy ways of expressing emotions without resorting to manipulative tactics.
- **Empathy Development:**
    - Focus on developing empathy and the ability to understand the emotions of others.

These individual therapy approaches are designed to enable the narcissistic leader to develop awareness of their own behavior and systematically make positive changes.

2. Group Therapy: Empathy, Support, and Social Skill Development

Group therapy provides a unique opportunity for the narcissistic leader to interact with other individuals in a safe and structural environment. The focus is on empathy, support, and the development of social skills.

Social-constructivist Therapy in Group Therapy:

Social-constructivist therapy emphasizes the social nature of personal experience and identity formation. For a narcissistic leader, this approach may include:

- **Perspective Sharing:**
  - Participation in conversations and activities enables the narcissistic leader to hear and understand the perspectives of others.
- **Empathic Interactions:**
  - Focus on developing empathy through interactions with other group members.
- **Social Skills Development:**
  - Opportunities to practice social skills, including listening, giving feedback, and communicating effectively.

This group therapy approach can make a valuable contribution to developing a more inclusive and empathetic approach to interpersonal relationships.

3. Narcissism: Practical Behavioral Change Guidelines

Narcissism coaching focuses specifically on developing practical skills and behavior change. It can be a valuable and direct approach that helps a narcissistic leader set specific goals and make change step by step.

Solution-centered coaching in narcissism coaching:

Solution-centered coaching places emphasis on purposefulness and systematic change. For a narcissistic leader, this approach may include:

- **Statement of Objective:**
    - Collaboration to set clear and achievable goals for personal growth and behavior change.
- **Step-by-step implementation:**
    - Identify small, feasible steps to facilitate behavior change.
- **Evaluation of Progress:**
    - Regular evaluation to measure the leader's progress and make adjustments to the plan where necessary.

This approach focuses on acquiring practical skills and promoting healthy behavior patterns.

4. Psychoeducation: Information and Understanding for Personal Growth

Psychoeducation provides information on narcissism, personal growth, and the impact of narcissistic behavior on individuals and the environment.

Courses and Workshops Based on Cognitive Behavioural Therapy (CBT) in Psychoeducation:

- **Awareness of Narcissism:**
  - Provide information on the characteristics of narcissism, including potential challenges and their impact on others.
- **Cognitive realignment:**
  - Integrate CRL principles to restructure negative thought patterns about narcissism.
- **Appropriate Practices:**
  - Offer practical guidelines and skills for dealing with narcissistic behavior, both for the narcissistic leader and those who interact with them.

Psychoeducation facilitates understanding and awareness and can play an essential role in promoting positive change.

5. Family Therapy: Restoring Relationships and Family Dynamics

Family therapy is critical, especially if the narcissistic leader's behavior has an impact on family ties. It provides a platform for the whole family to get involved in recovery.

Systemic therapy in family therapy:

- **Dynamics of the Family Understanding:**
  - Systemic therapy focuses on the complex interactions within a family and identifies possible dysfunctions.

- **Strengthening Communication:**
  - Facilitate healthy communication patterns within the family, including the narcissistic leader.
- **Individual responsibility:**
  - Promotes the adoption of individual responsibility and the development of family goals.

This therapy focuses on restoring family relationships and promoting a healthy family environment.

These models of counseling are designed to work collectively to provide a holistic approach to treating a narcissistic leader. Integrating individual, group, and family approaches can create a comprehensive framework to support narcissistic leaders in their journey of personal growth and behavior change.

How can you test yourself or ask family and friends to test you for possible Narcissistic tendencies?

Please remember that this evaluation is not a scientific or psychological measuring tool. You may use this tool or have your family or friends complete it on your behalf.

1. Empathy:

- How do you react when someone is emotional?
- Can you put yourself in other people's shoes and understand their perspective?
- Do you pay attention to the emotional needs of others in interactions?
- How do you feel when others succeed or experience difficulties?
- Are there times when you adjust your emotional response to better support others?

2. Self-awareness:

- Can you be honest about your own strengths and weaknesses?
- How do you deal with constructive criticism?
- Are there aspects of yourself you are aware of and want to improve?
- How do you describe yourself to others, and does this correspond to how others see you?
- How do you respond when you make mistakes?

3. Interpersonal Relationships:

- How do you maintain healthy relationships with family,

friends, and colleagues?

- Do you respect other people's ideas, even if they differ from yours?
- How do you support others' goals and accomplishments?
- Are there times when you have trouble maintaining harmony in relationships?
- How do you deal with conflict and try to find a positive solution?

4. Need for Admiration:

- How necessary is external approval to your sense of self-worth?
- How do you feel when you don't get the attention or admiration you want?
- Is there a pattern in which you try to present yourself as superior to others?
- Can you find self-affirmation and self-appreciation within yourself without looking for it from the outside?
- How do you deal with situations where others do not stop admiring you?

5. Critique Handling:

- How do you feel when someone directs criticism towards you?
- Can you distinguish objective criticism from subjective attacks?
- What do you do when you admit you were wrong or made a mistake?
- Is there a pattern in which you deal with criticism defensively?
- How do you deal with criticism from people you respect and trust?

6. Competitiveness:

- How do you deal with the success of others, especially if it contradicts your goals or achievements?
- Can you appreciate when others' success does not depend on your success?
- What is your reaction when someone performs better than you in a field?
- Are there times when you consider yourself to be better than others in general terms?
- How do you foster a climate of collaboration rather than competition?

7. Manipulative behavior:

- How do you deal with situations where you don't get your way?
- Can you communicate honestly without resorting to manipulative tactics?
- Is there a pattern in which you try to influence others' perceptions of you?
- How do you react when you notice others trying to manipulate you?
- How do you promote honesty and integrity in your interactions?

8. Introspection:

- How often do you take time for self-reflection on your own behavior?
- What is your purpose in self-reflection, and what changes have you made?
- Can you look objectively at your own motives and actions?

- Are there aspects of your behavior that you may be unaware of and need further consideration?
- How do you deal with discovering less pleasant aspects of yourself?

9. Responsibility:

- How do you accept responsibility for your own mistakes and actions?
- Are there times when you try to shift the blame for mistakes onto others?
- Can you acknowledge the impact of your actions on others and take responsibility for them?
- How do you deal with the consequences of mistakes you've made?
- How do you feel when someone else doesn't take responsibility?

10. Positive Influence:

- How do you try to have a positive impact on the lives of others?
- How do you support others' personal and professional goals?
- Is there a pattern in which you place your interests above those of others?
- How do you react when others don't have the same view as you?
- How do you create an environment in which others can thrive and grow?

These questions are designed to gain a deeper insight into various aspects of your behavior and self-esteem. It is essential to be honest and remember that no one is perfect. Self-development often involves accepting our strengths and weaknesses, as well as a constant pursuit of personal growth.

Please remember that only professional people can identify those deemed as narcissistic. Do not start testing every person you meet, your church leader or boss within your working environment, if they meet a few of the criteria explained in this book.

Don't miss out!

Visit the website below and you can sign up to receive emails whenever Carl Davis publishes a new book. There's no charge and no obligation.

https://books2read.com/r/B-A-ZAXZ-FVRTC

BOOKS 2 READ

Connecting independent readers to independent writers.

Also by Carl Davis

Ek, is Dawid Soeker
A Brief History Of Christianity In Africa
Icing the Eskimo - The Art of Aggressive Sales
Introduction to Pastoral Counselling
Nuclear Faith
Toxic Pulpit
Van Paradegrond tot Pastorie
Group Dynamics and Motivation
Introduction to Leadership and Management
Pastoral counselling models for perinatal and postpartum episodes
Basic New Testament Survey
Help! I'm managing personnel
So......You want to be a Waiter
The Art of Preaching
Eternal Logos: The Evolution of Scriptural Interpretation: From
Ancient Methodology to Postmodern Perspectives
Ewige Woord Die Evolusie van Skrifuitleg: Van Antieke Metodiek tot
Postmoderne Perspektiewe
Teaching Ministry
The Funny Side Of Reasoning - Fallacies, principles and typologies in
the modern business world.
Passion Unleashed: Igniting The Future With Purpose.

About the Author

Carl Davis holds a Doctorate in Missiology based upon research of Organizational Growth in the Post Modern Society.I started my work life serving in the South African Defence Force – first at the Recruiting Division, then moving to a Medical Command where I served as a Generalist Personnel Officer. For the last two years of my service, I was tasked with the Personnel management of the Integration process, inclusive of entrance and exit strategies.After honorable discharge after more than 10 years in the South African Defence Force, I took up the post of Managing Director of a Non-Government Organization, established to uplift impoverished communities in and around Potchefstroom, while also appointed as a part-time lecturer of undergraduates (specifically on leadership).Three years later I was appointed as Rector, managing an Educational Institute with 4000 students spread over 36 African countries. While in this position I had the opportunity to lecture extensively abroad and published various articles on leadership; with specific emphasis on motivation and group dynamics. I am a strong believer in utilizing a blended and integrated approach in all of the training (including the new material which I developed) I developed which included – Leadership (within a Faith based community), andragogy, and Cultural Diversity management.I am also a graduate of the University of Stellenbosch's Facilitative Leadership Programme (BUVTON), consulting and facilitating with organizations that are "stuck" (- Alice Mann 1998-) specifically in the process of change management.

www.ingramcontent.com/pod-product-compliance
Lightning Source LLC
Chambersburg PA
CBHW022142150726
47992CB00002B/723